Dispelling The Darkness:

Misconceptions Concerning Satan, The Occult, And The Dead

Edited and Compiled

By Greg W. Harmon

HP

Dispelling The Darkness:
Misconceptions Concerning Satan, The Occult, And The Dead

First Printing, December 1999

Published by:
Harmon House Publishing, Inc.
P.O. Box 2515
Bushnell, FL. 33513
(352) 568-8963

Cover Design By
William S. Howard

ISBN 0-9677022-0-8

Printed in the United States of America by Morris Publishing
3212 East Highway 30 • Kearney, Nebraska 68847 • 800-650-7888

Dedication

To The Bushnell Church of Christ, for allowing me to "grow in the grace and knowledge of our Lord and Savior Jesus Christ" (2 Peter 3:18).

Contributors To This Book

Darrell Conley. University of Texas, John Marshall Law School in Atlanta (B.S.). Presently enrolled in Master's program at Southern Christian University. After buying his first magic book at age 10, Darrell has had an interest in "honest deception." He has been a part-time magician since 1975. Darrell has attained the Order of Merlin for 25 continuous years of membership in the International Brotherhood of Magicians. He is a former officer in the Society of American Magicians. He is the author of several books, and is currently working with the Northern Oaks Church of Christ in San Antonio, Texas. He has been preaching for 45 years.

Bruce E. Daugherty. Freed-Hardeman University (B.A.). He has also taken graduate work from Southern Christian University and Harding University Graduate School of Religion. Bruce has worked on campaigns to Italy, Zambia and Botswana, Africa. He is a part-time Instructor for the Florida School of Preaching, and has been preaching for the Church of Christ in Daytona Beach, Florida since 1990. Bruce has been preaching for 22 years.

Thomas H. Holland. Freed Hardeman University, David Lipscomb University (B.A.), Abilene Christian University (M.A.), Southern Illinois University (Ph.D.). Tom is the author of 54 books. He spent 5 years as speaker on World Radio. He is currently dedicated to meeting work. Since 1950 he has preached in over 500 Gospel Meetings. Tom has been preaching the Gospel for 49 years.

Wayne Jackson. College of Evangelists. Sacramento Baptist College (B.A.), Southern Christian University (M.A.). He is the editor of

Christian Courier (Monthly Journal). Wayne is the author of 25 books. He is currently working with the Church of Christ in Stockton, California. Brother Jackson has been preaching for over 40 years. Wayne's chapter in this book was first published in *Reason & Revelation*, April 1998, pp. 25-31.

Howard Johnson. Graduate of the Florida School of Preaching; Bear Valley Bible Institute (B.Th.), and is currently working toward his Master's. Howard is the editor of *The Evangelist* (Monthly Journal), and the author of 3 books. He is currently working with the Church of Christ in Lake Butler, Florida. Howard has been preaching for 14 years.

Brian Kenyon. Florida Institute of Technology (A.S.), Florida School of Preaching, Freed Hardeman University (B.A) (M.A.). Brian has worked on campaigns in Scotland and three in Jamaica. He is currently a full-time Instructor at the Florida School of Preaching. He has been preaching for 9 years.

Denny Petrillo. York College (A.A.); Bear Valley School of Preaching; Harding University (B.A.); Harding Graduate School of Religion (M.A.); University of Nebraska (Ph.D.). He is currently Vice President of the *Bear Valley Bible Institute* (Denver, CO.). He is a Bible translator, and has done his seminar *"How we got the Bible"* on every Continent. Denny has been preaching for 22 years.

Bobby Simmons. Graduate of the Florida School of Preaching, Lael College and Graduate School (B.A.). Bobby has been on 2 campaigns to Jamaica. He is currently working with the Church of Christ in Bushnell, Florida. He has been preaching for 10 years.

Jackie M. Stearsman. Freed Hardeman University (A.A.), David Lipscomb University (B.A.), Harding Graduate School of Religion (M.A.). Jackie has taught for Michigan Christian College, and he is the current Director of the Florida School of Preaching. He is a regular speaker for Nationwide Lectureships. Jackie is also the author of many books and booklets. He has been preaching for over 30 years.

Dan Wheeler. Alabama Christian (A.A.), Western Illinois University (B.A.), University of Alabama (M.A.). Dan is working with the Church of Christ in Winter Park, Florida. He is also an Instructor for the University of Florida. Dan has preached for many Gospel Meetings and Lectureships.

Preface

The plans for this book began in October 1998. It was during the sixty-minute radio program, *Let Us Reason*, of which I am host. We were having a special series that month on the Occult. It dealt with many of the subjects that you will read about in this book. After the series was over, we received an overwhelming response by the listeners. We decided to put the programs in book form to give out to the public. However, there is so much that we didn't have time to say during the series that needed to be said. That's when the idea of a more in-depth book came to mind. When I began doing my research, I quickly realized that I was not qualified to write on these ever-changing topics. We were fortunate to obtain commitments from authors who *are* qualified to write chapters for this type of work.

In our world today, too many people have sought for answers in the wrong places. This book is designed to inform the public of why astrology, witchcraft, mediumship, etc., are wrong. It should be in no wise taken as an exhaustive work on the Occult, but more as a starting point for us to gain general information on these destructive subjects.

May this book be of value to you, the reader, and God forbid if a friend or loved one becomes entrapped with the Occult, may your informed mind be able to spot the evil, and then get them the help that they need.

- Greg W. Harmon
Editor & Compiler
November, 1999

Foreword

Robert Nisbet began a chapter of his 1948 publication Ideas Have Consequences with this observation about sensational journalism: "The rise of sensational journalism everywhere testifies to man's loss of points of reference, to his determination to enjoy the forbidden in the name of freedom" (Nisbet 29). Think for a moment about the expression: "man's loss of points of reference." As with navigation at sea, so with navigation in life. If a man loses his points of reference at sea, his way home is always in doubt, his hope of safe arrival at his destination is without factual basis. However much the safe arrival is desired does not change or remove the difficulty: Without legitimate points of reference, any course taken is taken by chance and by guesswork; it is liable (if not destined), in fact, to end in disaster!

It is here that this book seeks to bring critique, counsel, and direction. Modern man has in large measure lost his "points of reference;" now his is desperately trying to find new ones, hoping against hope they will bring him the same assurance and destiny as the old ones he has abandoned or renounced.

There is no denying the widespread abandonment or rejection of the old points of reference provided by faith in God, submission to Jesus Christ, and steadfast trust of Scripture as the word of God. From the painful embrace of evolution to the soul-chilling dance with post modernism and the consequent relativizing of all values, modern man has steadily spiraled downward from faith in God to a lack of faith in and an absence of trust in anything which has meaning and assurance beyond what is visible and what is bounded by the present moment!

As a footnote to the above, one may consider the words of Ernest Renan, a French skeptic of the past century. His own faith shattered and his writings seeking to remove the supernatural nature of Christ, his memory of what once was emerged in the words: "We are living on the perfume of an empty vase." The perfume of faith lingers, but the vase which once held it is now empty and the future can only be without the delight of the fragrance soon to drift away!

It is within this context that the particulars of the following chapters have their origin and purpose. In a quest for points of reference in a culture shot through with denial and skepticism of even the most sacred of religious beliefs and values, the fragrance from the empty vase still lingers. Ancient and more modern substitutes for genuine religious faith are quickly-reshuffled and dealt-again-from-the-bottom to a confused and restless age. The specific chapters (on topics from witches to speaking with the dead and hearing their rappings in a séance to tarot cards to black magic to ouija boards and planchettes to astrology to mediums and channeling, from false religions to modern denominationalism, and all the rest alluded to or discussed in detail) hold before the reader well written descriptions and critiques of these modern [although many have their origins in no-longer-remembered antiquity] substitutes for the way of God as revealed in Scripture. The fragrance from the past still lingers; but the source of this heart thrilling aroma of divine truth is rejected and the very best modern day substitutes cannot even come close to the original. Whatever the figure, the sadness of the modern world's plight comes through to all who know God in truth in Jesus.

Ancient Israel was admonished of God to have nothing to do with the various forms of the occult and spiritualism of their day. His words still ring with modern relevance:

> "When thou art come into the land which the LORD thy God giveth thee, thou shalt not learn to do after the abominations of those nations. There shall not be found among you any one that maketh his son or his

> daughter to pass through the fire, or that useth divination, or an observer of times, or an enchanter, or a witch, Or a charmer, or a consulter with familiar spirits, or a wizard, or a necromancer. For all that do these things are an abomination unto the LORD: and because of these abominations the LORD thy God doth drive them out from before thee. Thou shalt be perfect with the LORD thy God. For these nations, which thou shalt possess, hearkened unto observers of times, and unto diviners: but as for thee, the LORD thy God hath not suffered thee so to do" (Deut. 18:9-14).

In this interesting, informative, and well written book, one will find a series of exposures of the false ways of the current supposed religious and magical proposals many propound and too many embrace. The resolve is not merely to call attention to the errors and false ways of the views and fumblings discussed; there is the further and noble summons to leave such behind and allow the word of God to prevail as it did long ago in ancient Ephesus – filled at the time with various magical arts and devices. One reads:

> "Many also of them that had believed came, confessing, and declaring their deeds. And not a few of them that practised magical arts brought their books together and burned them in the sight of all; and they counted the price of them, and found it fifty thousand pieces of silver. So mightily grew the word of the Lord and prevailed" (Acts 19:18-20).

So, gentle reader, consider these words which expose as false and failing the fruitless searches by many today for what has never had substance although highly touted as legitimate substitutes for the truth of God – now often neglected and refused in much of the public square as well as the hearth – fires of homes. From the days of ancient Israel to the present moment, such false notions and attempts to read the supposed signs, understand the present, and tell the future have been abominations before God. May our generation also so regard them! May this book help each reader to come to this true awareness, and in such awareness turn anew to the word of God for guidance and assurance of his love and blessing now and forever.

-William Woodson, Th.D.
November 22, 1999

Nisbet, Robert. Ideas Have Consequences. Chicago: University of Chicago Press, 1984.

Table of Contents

Chapter 1

Astrology

Bruce E. Daugherty

Can you name something that is five thousand years old, yet it is read on a daily basis worldwide by more people than is the Bible? You are correct if you guessed the horoscope. Many people dismiss it as a fad or a curiosity. It is looked upon as harmless or something to pass the time in a Chinese restaurant. Yet we are not surprised when we hear of important people who read their horoscope. Entertainers, athletes, even politicians regularly consult their astrologists and horoscopes. Though once on the decline, the consultation of horoscopes and astrologists was boosted in 1988 with the report in *People* Magazine that President Ronald Reagan and his wife Nancy made important daily decisions after consulting their astrologist in California (Wadler 107). Increased interest in astrology is seen in the inclusion of the horoscope in the daily newspapers and the many sites on the Internet that offer information concerning how to live in harmony with the cosmos.

The Bible encourages the "proving" or testing of all things (1 Thessalonians 5:17). This includes astrology. Do the stars direct our future? Does the Bible have anything to say about whether Christians should be consulting horoscopes?

DEFINING TERMS

Astrology is the study of how events on earth correspond to the positions and movements of astronomical bodies, particularly the sun, moon, planets and stars ("Astrology"). It studies and interprets the system of constant relations between the cosmos and the earth, between the stars and man, for the purpose of predicting earthly events and human behavior ("Astrologia").

It is important from the outset to differentiate astrology from the science of astronomy. According to *Webster's New World Dictionary*, astronomy is the system of physical laws by which the stars, planets, and all other heavenly bodies are observed to function (86). As a science, astronomy deals with the composition, size, motion and relative position of these bodies in space. But astronomy makes no speculation or claims that these bodies have a relationship or correspondence to earthly inhabitants or their activities.

An important term to also understand is horoscope. A horoscope is an astrological forecast based upon an individual's zodiacal chart (Ibid. 677). This chart is based upon the 12 months of the calendar year or based upon a 12-year cycle as practiced by the Chinese.

Associated with the horoscope is the zodiac. The zodiac is an imaginary belt in the heavens extending for about eight degrees on either side of the apparent path of the sun and including the paths of the moon and principal planets; it is divided into twelve equal parts, or signs, each named for a different constellation (Ibid. 1654). It should not be surprising that astrology and the reading of horoscopes are so prevalent in our society today. The philosophic basis for astrology is very compatible with modern man. Modern man has made a rejection of reasoned religion, but cannot free himself of superstitions. The modern is cynical enough to sneer and mock anything he cannot see or understand but is gullible enough to read the horoscope or consult an astrologist (Hodge, Jr. 41). Like practitioners in animist cultures, astrologists seek to know the future, to control their destinies, to live in harmony with the planets. With this type of thinking, man is a made a slave of determinism or fate; therefore, man is not to blame; man is not responsible for his actions. Man, when viewed from this perspective is the pawn of the fatalistic forces of the universe. Therefore man has no sin and, no need for salvation from sin.

AN ANCIENT PRACTICE

The history of astrology is extensive. It seems to have developed independently in many different civilizations: the ancient Egyptians, Babylonians, Chinese, Hindu's, and Mayans all practiced forms of astrology. The earliest discovery of astrology dates as early as 3000 BC. The stars and the heavenly bodies were worshiped together with the idolatrous beliefs of polytheism.

Originally, it is believed the ancients made observations of the sun, moon, and positions of the stars and made records of the change of seasons. These records were important to the planting of crops, especially to anticipate seasons of rain. From this ability to associate the locations of the heavenly bodies with the seasons and changes in climate, the study of the heavenly bodies expanded to a broader system by which predictions of the future and human behavior were made based upon the movements of the sun, moon, and the planets. The ancient practice of astrology was related to divination. Divination takes its name from its primary root, literally meaning "a divider." There were (and still are) an infinite variety of practices by which men sought to gain knowledge of the future by some independent, arbitrary means: divination and astrology were just two of those methods. Ezekiel 21:21 describes Nebuchadnezzar's use of divination: "For the king of Babylon stood at the parting of the way, at the head of the two ways, to use divination: he shook the arrows to and fro, he consulted the teraphim, he looked in the liver." The liver of a sacrificial offering was divided into portions and the "diviner" was then consulted. The liver was believed to be the internal organ that was the seat of the victim's life. By looking at its divisions the "diviner" determined what the "god" to whom the animal had been sacrificed revealed of his will. The "looking into the liver" was one way for understanding what the believer was to choose. An astrologer "divided the heavens" to determine the will of the "gods" or the stars and then accordingly, predicted the future ("Astrology 2"). The modern practice of astrology still reflects this "dividing" nature: at the birth of an individual, a chart of the heavens will be made. This chart will be divided into 12 sections, representing the signs of the zodiac on their elliptic path. The planets, the sun, and the moon are assigned to the 12 divisions at the time the horoscope is cast. Each of these planets is believed to represent basic human drives and characteristics. Further divisions are also made assigning 12 houses which corresponds to the 24-hour period in which the earth rotates once on its axis. Each house deals with certain areas of a person's life, such as marriage, health, work, travel and death. Astrologists make predictions by interpreting the position of the planetary bodies within the divisions of the horoscope.

Alexander the Great's conquest of Persia, brought the practice of astrology into contact with the Greek world. In the hands of the Greeks, most notably Pythagoras and Plato, astrology appeared less an oriental religion and took on the respectability of a science. This respectability as a science continued into Medieval times, despite intense opposition from Roman Catholicism. During the early period of the Renaissance, astrology maintained a position of prestige and counted among its practitioners Johann Kepler. As the universe became better known through the observations of Copernicus and Galileo, however, astrology began to decline. In the eighteenth and nineteenth centuries astrology was discredited as a science and was relegated to the margins of societal acceptance, mainly due to the rejection of its philosophic basis in determinism. Only in the twentieth century has there been a change in the view of astrology, primarily through the psychological theories of Carl Jung and the statistical methods of Choisnard and von Klocker.

BIBLICAL PROHIBITIONS TO ASTROLOGY

Despite claims of astrologists (Dixon 436), the Bible is not compatible with astrology. The Old Testament was consistent in its condemnation of all idolatrous related practices: augury, sooth-saying, divination, etc. "Lest ye corrupt yourselves, and make you a graven image in the form of any figure, the likeness of male or female, the likeness of any beast that is on the earth, the likeness of any winged bird that flieth in the heavens, the likeness of anything that creepeth on the ground, the likeness of any fish that is in the water under the earth; and lest thou lift up thine eyes unto heaven, and when thou seest the sun and the moon and the stars, even all the host of heaven, thou be drawn away and worship them, and serve them, which Jehovah thy God hath allotted unto all the peoples under the whole heaven" (Deuteronomy 4:16-19). To worship and serve the sun, moon, and stars would include being guided by them!

"When thou art come into the land which Jehovah thy God giveth thee, thou shalt not learn to do after the abominations of those nations. There shall not be found with thee any one that maketh his son or his daughter to pass through the fire, one that useth divination, one that practiseth augury, or an enchanter, or a sorcerer, or a charmer, or a consulter with a familiar spirit, or a wizard, or a necromancer. For whosoever doeth these things is an abomination unto Jehovah: and because of these abominations Jehovah thy God doth drive them out from before thee. Thou shalt be perfect with Jehovah thy God. For these nations, that thou shalt dispossess, hearken unto them that practise augury, and unto diviners; but as for thee, Jehovah thy God hath not suffered thee so to do" (Duet. 18:9-14). Though astrology is not mentioned specifically in this text, it's association with divination has already been established. Texts that condemn divination include a condemnation of the practices of astrology.

"Stand now with thine enchantments, and with the multitude of thy sorceries, wherein thou hast labored from thy youth; if so be thou shalt be able to profit, if so be thou mayest prevail. Thou art wearied in the multitude of thy counsels: let now the astrologers, the star-gazers, the monthly prognosticators, stand up, and save thee from the things that shall come upon thee. Behold, they shall be as stubble; the fire shall burn them; they shall not deliver themselves from the power of the flame: it shall not be a coal to warm at, nor a fire to sit before. Thus shall the things be unto thee wherein thou hast labored: they that have trafficked with thee from thy youth shall wander every one to his quarter; there shall be none to save thee" (Isaiah 47:12-15). In this passage, God sarcastically challenges the astrologers to be able to do anything to save the people from their coming punishment due to their idolatry.

"Hear ye the word which Jehovah speaketh unto you, O house of Israel: thus saith Jehovah, Learn not the way of the nations, and be not dismayed at the signs of heaven; for the nations are dismayed at them. For the customs of the peoples are vanity; for one cutteth a tree out of the forest, the work of the hands of the workman with the axe. They deck it with silver and with gold; they fasten it with nails and with hammers, that it move not. They are like a palm-tree, of turned work, and speak not: they must needs be borne, because they cannot go. Be not afraid of them; for they cannot do evil, neither is it in them to do good" (Jeremiah 10:1-5). In this passage, Jeremiah warns the people to turn from their practice of following the customs of the nations that surrounded them. Included in this prohibition was the encouragement to not be worried by the "signs of heaven" - clearly a reference to the world of astrology. God's people were told to not be afraid of the "signs" and the idols, because they could do neither evil nor good! People today must realize there is no benefit to astrology!

Not only does the Bible contain warnings against astrology, but it also contains an amazing admission from astrologers concerning the limits of astrology. Astrologers of the court of Nebuchadnezzar in Babylon were unable to interpret the king's dream without having any idea about what the king had dreamed. When pressed by the king to relate the dream and its meaning the court astrologer admitted their limitations: "The Chaldeans answered before the king, and said, There is not a man upon the earth that can show the king's matter, forasmuch as no king, lord, or ruler, hath asked such a thing of any magician, or enchanter, or Chaldean. And it is a rare thing that the king requireth, and there is no other that can show it before the king, except the gods, whose dwelling is not with flesh" (Daniel 2:10-11). When Daniel could provide the dream and its meaning, he makes it clear that it was God who gave him the information, not any horoscope! "Daniel answered before the king, and said, The secret which the king heath demanded can neither wise men, enchanters, magicians, nor soothsayers, show unto the king; but there is a God in heaven that revealeth secrets, and he hath made known to the king Nebuchadnezzar what shall be in the latter days. Thy dream, and the visions of thy head upon thy bed, are these: as for thee, O king, thy thoughts came [into thy mind] upon thy bed, what should come to pass hereafter; and he that revealeth secrets hath made known to thee what shall come to pass. But as for me, this secret is not revealed to me for any wisdom that I have more than any living, but to the intent that the interpretation may be made known to the king, and that thou mayest know the thoughts of thy heart" (Daniel 2:27-30).

Turning to the pages of the New Testament, the Bible is consistent in its stance toward astrology and related practices. Stephen quotes from Amos in his speech before the Sanhedrin. That quotation brings to light Israel's idolatry during the wilderness wanderings following their deliverance from Egyptian bondage. "But God turned, and gave them up to serve the host of heaven; as it is written in the book of the prophets, Did ye offer unto me slain beasts and sacrifices Forty years in the wilderness, O house of Israel? And ye took up the tabernacle of Moloch, And the star of the god Rephan, The figures which ye made to worship them: And I will carry you away beyond Babylon" (Acts 7: 42-43). The text specifically says that God gave up on those who were determined to practice idolatry and this included serving "the host of heaven." The wilderness period included the idolatrous worship of Moloch and Rephan, both idolatrous deities associated with the constellation of Taurus and the planet Saturn.

The book of Acts also tells of the casting out of a demon from a slave girl by Paul. "And it came to pass, as we were going to the place of prayer, that a certain maid having a spirit of divination met us, who brought her masters much gain by soothsaying. The same following after Paul and us cried out, saying, These men are servants of the Most High God, who proclaim unto you the way of salvation. And this she did for many days. But Paul, being sore troubled, turned and said to the spirit, I charge thee in the name of Jesus Christ to come out of her. And it came out that very hour" (Acts 16:16-18). If astrology and divination were compatible with Christianity, Paul would not have healed this young woman! Another incident recorded in the book of Acts reveals the clear incompatibility between Christianity and the practices of the pagan world. "And not a few of them that practiced magical arts brought their books together and burned them in the sight of all; and they counted the price of them, and found it fifty thousand pieces of silver" (Acts 19:19). Again, although the words astrology, horoscope and zodiac are not mentioned specifically in this text, it is more than likely that the "magic arts" and the books mentioned in this verse included almanacs and zodiacal tables necessary to the practice of astrology.

This testimony from Scripture should make it very plain that Christians cannot and must not consult astrologers and horoscopes. Astrology is referred to in the Bible, but it is always condemned. Astrology is a repudiation of God as it assigns God's powers to the creation rather than the Creator! Christians do not need to consult astrologers and the stars to know God's will. They can know the will of God through faith, a faith that is rational and credible. This faith is what the Apostle Paul had when he spoke to his fellow travelers on the ship in the Mediterranean sea: "Wherefore, sirs, be of good cheer: for I believe God, that it shall be even so as it hath been spoken unto me" (Acts 27:25). We have that same kind of faith today when we believe the written word of God, that it shall be exactly as God promised. It was this faith that Paul commended in Timothy: "And that from a babe thou hast known the sacred writings which are able to make thee wise unto salvation through faith which is in Christ Jesus" (2 Tim. 3:15). Salvation is by faith in Christ Jesus and the source of that faith is scripture. What is needed are not the charts and horoscopes of astrologers. All that is needed is to believe the testimony of the Bible!

ASTROLOGY'S SCIENTIFIC BANKRUPTCY

Since the sixteenth century, scientists have rejected the claims and foundations of astrology. Thanks to the work begun by Copernicus and Galileo, science has rejected the principles of astrology. In 1975 more than 186 prominent American scientists gathered to denounce "the pretentious claims of astrological charlatans" as they spoke of astrology's scientific bankruptcy (McDowell and Stewart 161). The following are just a few of the scientific contradictions inherent in astrology.

Scientists reject astrology because they know that the divisions of the heavens set by the ancients were purely arbitrary: there was no reason or logic for the divisions they made. Zodiac "signs" and "astrological houses" are purely imaginary constructs and have nothing corresponding to them in nature. The elaborate "systems" developed by astrologers are non-observable and therefore, non-scientific.

Scientists reject astrology because they know it is based on ancient assumptions that have since proven to be false. Astrology began with the assumption that the earth is the center of our planetary system. Dating from the time of Ptolemy and continuing through the Medieval period, "geocentricity" was commonly believed and even dogmatically asserted. The observations of Copernicus and Galileo proved the sun to be the center of our system and destroyed the credibility of astrology.

The repudiation of astrology as a science has continued with the discovery of other planets in our solar system. The ancient observers of the heavens were limited in their view: they were able to see five planets, and the sun and the moon. This made a total of seven, the number which is usually used to make a horoscope. Yet if the theories of astrology are correct in their assertions that the planets have a bearing on human activity, then the three missing planets also influence human events. But most horoscopes do not consider these planets at all. How can these horoscopes be accurate if they do not consider all the planets? (McDowell and Stewart 163).

Another major scientific problem for astrology is the shifting of the constellations. Ancient observers of the heavens were not aware that the constellations were changing. Due to the fact of shifting in the constellations, the heavens resemble a different configuration today than what they did 2000 years ago. This changes the entire nature of the zodiac. How accurate can a horoscope be if Leo is now in the sign of Virgo?

EXPLAINING THE APPARENT ACCURACY OF ASTROLOGY

Despite the evidence of astrology's lack of real credibility many people continue to place their faith in astrology. Often, the reason given for this faith is pragmatic. For these individuals, astrology works, whether there is any logical or scientific evidence for it. But there are other reasons for this supposed accuracy. One of those reasons is the ambiguous and general nature of the "predictions" given. For example, here is a horoscope copied from *Daytona Beach News-Journal*, January 23, 1999:

> "Be careful that you're not perceived by friends as putting your interests and needs above everybody else's today. They'll resent it if they think you're trying to manipulate them."

This is a piece of advice, not a prediction. It would generally be true for any and every day of the year, for any and every situation one could find. Since it is given for the specific date of January 23, 1999 is it okay for me to be perceived as manipulating others on other days of the year? It should also be noted, this horoscope in the local paper carries the following disclaimer: " . . . should be read for entertainment value only. Such predictions have no reliable basis in scientific fact."

Another factor in the supposed accuracy of astrology is that its predictions are made so that whatever the outcome of an event, the astrologer is covered. Note this observation:

> "There are so many variables and options to play with that the astrologer is always right. Break a leg when your astrologer told you the signs were good, and he can congratulate you on escaping what might have happened had the signs been bad. Conversely, if you go against the signs and nothing happens, the astrologer can insist that you were subconsciously careful because you had been forewarned" (Time 56).

A final consideration concerning astrology's pragmatic value is the predisposition to believe by the practitioner. Just like the success of psychics and faith healers, the true story of astrological success lies more in the psychological makeup of the individual rather than the accuracy of the stars.

CONSEQUENCES TO ACCEPTING ASTROLOGY'S PREMISE

There are consequences to accepting the philosophic assumptions of astrology. Any belief system that would rob an individual of their free will should be avoided. The resulting hopelessness and despair are too great an exchange to be made for the freedom, hope and liberty that Jesus offers. It has often been pointed out that astrology makes slaves of its believers as man is reduced to being a mere pawn in the universe. But it also needs to be pointed out such a system makes an individual a slave and a pawn of those astrologers who would manipulate believers for financial gain or for other motives. We should not take lightly or call harmless anything that God condemned as an "abomination" or that has the potential to so enslave.

Astrology is Biblically condemned and scientifically bankrupt. May we allow the truth to set us free (John 8:32) and may we follow the instructions given long ago:

> "Seek him that maketh the seven stars and Orion, and turneth the shadow of death into the morning, and maketh the day dark with night: that calleth for the waters of the sea, and poureth them out upon the face of the earth: The LORD is his name" (Amos 5:8).

WHAT ABOUT THE WISE MEN AND THE BIRTH OF JESUS?

The narrative of the wise men who came seeking the newborn king of the Jews has often been referred to by astrologists as proof of the legitimacy of astrology and as proof of its compatibility with Christianity. A current astrology web page declares:

> "The gospel according to St. Matthew tells the story of the three wise men, known as the Magi. Many theological experts have declared these Magi to be astrologers, to whom the star in the east was a major astrological sign. Matthew described this magnificent star which guided the Magi to the Christ. The Magi, according to other historical writings, were unsurpassed in their wisdom and knowledge of things luminous. It was, in fact, one of the Persian Magi who predicted the birth of Christ. The star of Bethlehem, of course, foretold the birth of Christ" (Astrologynow).

The assumptions of this website article are many. It contains a number of inaccuracies as well as assertions, which cannot be proven.

Who were the Magi? The word was originally indicative of the priest caste of the Medes and Persians. These individuals were students of nature, astrology, medicine and learning of various sources. They functioned as advisors and religious intercessors for pagan kings. The title was given to the Jewish captive, Daniel. "Then the king made Daniel great, and gave him many great gifts, and made him to rule over the whole province of Babylon, and to be chief governor over all the wise men "of Babylon" (Daniel 2:48). Later usage of the word then reveals that it came to be applied to all individuals who devoted themselves to such learning, whether they were astrologers or not! The visitors who sought the king of the Jews and worshipped Him with gifts were students of the stars, probably astrologers. "However, their presence in the biblical record is not a divine endorsement of astrology" (Wiersbe 14). There are many things which are mentioned in the Bible, but which do not have God's approval. By the fallacious reasoning of this website writer one could suppose that God approves of Satan, since Satan is included in the Bible.

Nowhere does the text say Matthew described the star. These men were not fascinated with the star but with the One the star led them to. All that the text says was that the Magi had seen the star in the east, that somehow they associated it with the birth of a king of the Jewish people, and that the star reappeared after they had inquired about the new king's birth in Jerusalem at the court of Herod.

How had God indicated to the Magi that this star signified the birth of "the king of the Jews?" The answer to this question is unclear and no conjecture can be dogmatically asserted. As students of the stars, the appearance alone of a unique star could have been enough to compel these men to leave their homes in the East and travel to the land of Judah.

Others have put forth the fact that Balaam's prophecy of old (Numbers 23:17) could have been retained in Mesopotamian knowledge. With the ascendancy of Daniel and Daniel's God Jehovah in the estimation of these pagan learned men, this prophecy could have had more significance to these men and compelled them to journey to Judah to view its fulfillment. Others have put forth their criticisms of this theory, believing it would not be reasonable that an obscure text alone for all those centuries would have motivated the Magi into making their trip.

Another theory put forth as to how God revealed the birth of the Christ to these Gentiles was that He did so by a dream. The text tells us that God divinely forewarned them in a dream of Herod's murderous intent and directed them on another route to their homes. Though the text does not explicitly state how they associated the star with the king of the Jews, it is not an unreasonable to conjecture to suppose that they were advised by a dream to make their journey.

Why had God given this special sign to the Magi? Simply, they represented the Gentiles who were to be beneficiaries of the coming of the Messiah, as foretold in prophecy. "And it shall come to pass in that day, that the root of Jesse, that standeth for an ensign of the peoples, unto him shall the nations seek; and his resting place shall be glorious" (Isaiah 11:10. See also Isaiah 60:1-6). This root out of Jesse was a figurative term to describe the Messiah. The entire ministry of Jesus, from birth to death, would be marked by Gentiles who sought Jesus and in turn His blessings would include them. " And that the Gentiles might glorify God for his mercy; as it is written, Therefore will I give praise unto thee among the Gentiles, and sing unto thy name. And again he saith, Rejoice, ye Gentiles, with his people. And again, Praise the Lord, all ye Gentiles; And let all the peoples praise him. And again, Isaiah saith, There shall be the root of Jesse, And he that ariseth to rule over the Gentiles; On him shall the Gentiles hope. Now the God of hope fill you with all joy and peace in believing, that ye may abound in hope, in the power of the Holy Spirit" (Romans 15:9-13). The inclusion of the Magi in the account of Matthew does not prove the legitimacy of astrology. Instead it was the fulfillment of prophecy which indicated a merciful God who desired all men to be saved. "And He made of one every nation of men to dwell on all the face of the earth, having determined their appointed seasons, and the bounds of their habitation; that they should seek God, if haply they might feel after Him and find Him, though He is not far from each one of us: for in him we live, and move, and have our being; as certain even of your own poets have said, For we are also his offspring" (Acts 17:26-28). In fact, the inclusion of the Magi as the Holy Spirit guided Matthew demonstrated the inadequacy of astrology!

> "Precisely since they are Gentiles, they receive their proclamation through nature (see Romans 1:19-20; 2:14-15); but, like Balaam of old who also came from the East and was endowed with special insight, they recognize the salvific import of the Davidic star. Although they hasten to Jerusalem to pay homage, the full revelation of the Messiah cannot be gleaned from nature: it is a secret found in the Scriptures, the special revelation that God has given to the Jews alone. And so the magi must learn from the Jewish Scriptures God's plan of salvation before they can find the Messiah and pay him homage" (Brown 182).

If we would be wise today, it is not because we follow the stars, but that we seek and worship "the King of Kings and Lord of Lords."

WORKS CITED

"Astrologia." Religioni e Miti Dizionario Enciclopedia, vol I. Milan, Italy: Bompiani Editori, 1984.

AstrologyNow. The Christian Bible and Astrology. Internet. 1999. http://astrologynow.com/astrology.201.htm

"Astrology: Fad and Phenomenon." Time Magazine, March 21, 1969: 47-56.

"Astrology." Microsoft Encarta, 1994 Edition.

"Astrology 2." International Standard Bible Encyclopedia, Vol. I. Grand Rapids: Eerdman's Publishing, 1953. Reprint.

Brown, Raymond E. The Birth and Death of the Messiah. New York: Anchor Bible Reference Library, Doubleday Publishers, 1993.

Clarke, Adam. Clarke's Commentary, Matthew-Revelation. Nashville: Abingdon Press, reprint of 1832 edition.

Dixon, Jeanne. Yesterday, Today, and Forever. New York: William Morrow and Company, Inc. 1975.

Hodge, Charles B. A Biblical Study of Satan. Dallas: Gospel Teachers Publications, 1973.

McDowell, Josh and Stewart, Don. Handbook of Today's Religions. Nashville: Thomas Nelson Publishers, 1983.

Wadler, Joyce with Angela Blessing, Dirk Mathison, and Margie Bonnett Sellinger. "The President's Astrologers." People Magazine, May 23, 1988: 106-113.

Wiersbe, Warren. The Bible Exposition Commentary, Vol. I. Wheaton: Victor Books, 1989

Chapter 2

The History of Satan

Thomas H. Holland

Any objective observer of the world scene, of the culture's condition, knows the reality of what a former U. S. Senator identified as "man's inhumanity to man." Wars, sexual immorality with spread of venereal diseases, babies born out of wedlock, broken homes and dashed dreams, murder, robbery, rape, lying, cheating, deceit, anger, abuse of the young, and abuse of the elderly, are all problems which daily plaque society. Pages of history are almost dripping blood that mankind has shed through wars.

Surely, something or someone, has and has had a profoundly significant influence on the minds of people. What is that influence, or who is that powerful influence? Is there a sinister force at work among people? Is that negative force personified as "the devil, Satan"? Or, is there a being, a shrewd, intelligent, manipulative being whose name is "Satan" and who is often identified as "the devil"?

The answer to the identification of the influence of evil may provide information that can help us in the daily struggle with forces in life that can rob us of purity of heart, peace of mind, and the pursuit of a quality of life which prompts us to be good and to do good, thereby developing a character that would be comfortable "at home" with God and in His Holy presence.

It would be difficult to exaggerate the importance of a study about Satan, the devil; because, this study actually is an exploration of the origin and nature of evil. There is more than a philosophical challenge in this study of Satan. There is a personal concern for sincere students of Scripture. Did a Good, Gracious, Holy God create evil--the antithesis of His Goodness? If not, from whence came evil? If evil originated in heaven, could it happen again and what guarantee do we have that the beauty of God's eternal abode of the righteous will not be marred by evil?

Evidently, many people have difficulty accepting the personality and consequently, the reality of the devil. To some, Satan is but the personification of evil, not a person of evil. Belief in a personal Satan would be viewed as the belief of a myth.

Many years ago, some people concluded that the devil had died. In October, 1850, Jacob Creath, Jr. wrote to the Millennial Harbinger about the existence of "the Old Serpent--the Devil." Creath said:

> "I find, in traveling over the country, there are persons who doubt his existence; and even some of our brethren are skeptical about his still being in existence. If you have heard of his death, or his annihilation, or of his disappearance from the dominions of God, please inform us through your periodical *when* and *what* the old gentleman died, and where he is buried."

The denial of the reality of the devil today comes from people who have difficulty accepting the Bible as the verbally inspired word of God. R. C. Foster identified these people as "modernists." He said:

> "The Modernist deny the existence of demons as they do that of angels. Their denial of the existence of the devil and of God is only the natural extreme of their rejection of the repeated accounts in the Scriptures of the works of the devil and his demons" (Foster 415)

Unfortunately,

> "Most of the common notions (about the devil), are drawn from mere tradition, popularized in England by Milton, but

without even a vestige of Scriptural authority" (McClintock 9:363)

Much superstition and uncontrolled imagination have resulted in the picture of the devil as a type of cartoon character, a being with a sinister look of his face, a forked tail extending from his red suited body, horns protruding from his head, while he holds a pitchfork in his hands.

This depiction of the devil is unfortunate. If such a creature walked down the streets, most intelligent people would probably flee for safety.

The only valid, reliable source of information about the devil is in the Bible, the word of God. God's word identifies the devil, gives insights relative to his origin, explains the sins or designs of Satan and reveals his final doom.

Some today evidently believe that belief in the reality of Satan, the devil, is actually a revelation of one's failure to intellectually "grow up." Allen Webster quoted someone as saying, "belief in a personal Satan is part of mankind's nursery furniture."

CLARIFICATION BY IDENTIFICATION

There are two prominent names for the devil revealed in the Bible and there are several descriptive expressions which give insight into his nature and designs.

The name "Satan" is used in Scripture some forty times. If one traces the etymology of the name "Satan," he will discover that the name is derived from a verb, "which means, 'to lie in wait, 'to oppose', 'to be an adversary'; hence, the noun denotes an adversary, or opposer" (McClintock 9:360).

Another name by which Satan is identified is "Devil." One finds this identification about fifty times in the New Testament. "'Devil' is transferred from the verb (which means), 'to thrust through', 'to carry over', 'to inform against, 'to accuse'" (Ibid 9:361).

The conclusion is: "'Satan' expresses his character as an opposer of all good.... 'Devil' denotes more particularly the relation which he bears to the saints, as their traducer and accuser" (Ibid 9:361)

The devil indeed is the "accuser." He certainly slandered God by telling Eve that God was deliberately withholding something that would enhance her life. The devil even had the audacity to accuse God of lying. God had said, "You shall not eat of it, neither shall you touch it, lest you die" (Genesis 3:3).

The devil said, "You shall not surely die" (Gen. 3:4).

Bible scholars date the book of Job as belonging to the Genesis era. If this is so, then near the dawn of man's existence, the devil not only slandered a Good, Gracious God, but he falsely accused a good and righteous man, Job (Job 1).

The devil, the "accuser of our brethren is cast down, which accused them before our God day and night" (Rev. 12:10).

The apostle Peter used both identifications when he wrote: "Be sober, be vigilant; because your adversary the devil as a roaring lion, walketh about, seeking whom he may devour" (I Pet. 5:8).

In addition to these two prominent names in the Scriptures, there are several descriptive (and therefore informative) designations of the devil.

He is identified as "the tempter' (Matt. 4:3). He is also called "the devil," (Matt. 4:5; 4:10). Jesus called "the tempter", Satan (Matt. 4:10). As a "tempter," he deliberately attempts to get people to sin against God.

If the "Devil" is just the personification of evil, or a personification of "the principle of evil," then Jesus was not tempted by a reality or a real personal being, rather he was only tempted by the "evil principle." If that is the case, then in whom did the "principle of evil" reside? In Jesus? If so, was He, or is He, the sinless Son of God?

Jesus said that Satan is "the father of lies" (John 8:44). But, the problem remains: How could a "principle of evil" tell a lie?

The Lord also identified the devil as a "murderer" (John 8:44). In a real sense, Satan murdered Adam and Eve and all of those through the centuries who have died. "Murderer' (manslayer) attributes to the devil far more than the physical murders that are committed by men; it charges him with bringing death in all its destructive power upon the whole of mankind" (Lenski 650).

Our Lord also identified the devil as "the prince (ruler) of this world" (John 12:31). The death of our Savior "destroyed" the control of the devil (Heb. 2:9-12). Now, the only subjects, or slaves, that the devil claims are those who are willing for him to dominate and destroy them. God's redeemed children can indeed "resist the devil" (James 4.8). Woods observed:

> "Satan is called 'the prince of this world' because the world has been his domain from the time of the fall in Eden... His domination of men was to be broken and ultimately fail... Jesus wrested from Satan's power over sin, death and the grave by his death and triumphant resurrection... Satan's reign began to decline at Calvary and it will be totally terminated at the end of the age" (Woods 267,268)

The apostle Paul identified the devil as "the god of this world (age)" (II Cor. 4:4). The "world" or "age" identifies the mass of mankind who let the devil have control of their lives and consequently, their destinies. The line made popular by a television comic, "The devil made me do it," may have communicated more truth than humor!

The names and descriptive titles of the devil surely gives us valuable information about his nature and efforts to hurt mankind.

How could people become, as they sometimes identify themselves, "devil worshippers"? Surely, it must reveal the essence of ignorance for people to offer worship to one who seeks to deceive and destroy them!

Considering the pain and woe that the "murderer" has inflicted on the human race, how could any of us listen to "the father of lies" when he tries to convince us that God is not good and that He is actually denying us, through His restrictive commandments, the "good life"? It is no compliment to our intelligence to embrace the lies of the devil.

How can God's children who by an obedient faith have escaped the domain of the devil, those redeemed or set free from Satan's service and the devil's domination over their lives and destinies, how can they go back to the slavery and potential eternal death? (Col. 1:12-14; II Pet. 1:3,4; 2:20-22). Saints of God who surrender to Satan do not compliment their intelligence nor their spiritual manhood or womanhood. What caused their spiritual resistance to get low? (James 4:8).

THE DEVIL'S "DEVISES" AND "WILES"

Strength and safety from Satan's deception demands a knowledge of his "devices" (II Cor. 2:11). The word translated "device" means that which has been "thought out." "Devise" means "plots", "evil schemings." The word signifies the functions of the intellective faculty" (Rogers and Rogers 396)

The "wiles" of the Devil (Eph. 6:11), identifies his "scheming, craftiness" (Ibid 446)

Satan has his "schemes," his "thought out plots." Underestimating his cunning power renders one unprepared for the inevitable "evil day" (Eph. 6:13). The necessity of taking God's "whole armor" (Eph. 6:11) is imperative if one hopes to "stand against the wiles (schemes, plots) in the evil day" (Eph. 6:11,13).

Perhaps the identity of some of Satan's "fiery darts" will help us prepare for the inevitable spiritual conflict.

One deadly "fiery dart" is ***doubt***. In Satan's first effort to get people to reject God, the adversary used doubt. Satan succeeded in getting Eve to doubt that God meant what He had said. Satan denied God's word. God had said, "Eat (of the forbidden fruit) and you will surely die" (Gen. 3:3). Satan said to Eve, "You will *not* surely die" (Gen. 3:4).

Satan convinced her that God was not good because He had withheld from Eve something that would enhance her life. Indeed, she would "be like God knowing good and evil" (Gen. 3:5).

Once the doubt that God meant what He said had been established, then Eve could look upon the forbidden fruit as a thing to be desired. At this point she has fallen victim to Satan's scheme. She is not concerned about the consequence of disobeying God. She is finding the forbidden fruit "a desirable thing" and the desire is reinforced by the idea that she will find satisfaction for a new and exciting dimension of her life.

Through the centuries even until this present hour, people are victims of the "fiery dart" of **doubt.** If Satan can get us to doubt God's word, if he can succeed in getting us to question whether or not God means what He has said, then he knows that he is winning the battle for our allegiance to him, and therefore, our rejection of God's rightful place in our lives.

How does Satan create doubt today? He "fashions himself into an angel of light" (II Cor. 11:14). He has already deceived enough people that they gladly serve him in creating doubt in minds of men.

Some of Satan's effective servants occupy professor's chairs in institutions devoted to education. There was a time when "educate" meant "developing the minds and the morals." Those who have been exposed to modem education have heard, "Once you are educated you can cast off faith."

Some of Satan's servants wear religious garb. They question the miracles recorded in the Bible, and therefore, question the veracity of Scripture.

Some "scholars" are so "brilliant" that they can go through the record of Jesus' life recorded by Matthew, Mark, Luke, and John, and can assert, "Jesus said this," but "Jesus didn't say what Matthew, Mark, Luke and John have quoted him as having said."

Satan's servants sometimes assert, "The Bible is full of contradictions." The implication of this charge, relativism not withstanding, is that truth must be consistent. If there is a reasonable explanation of an alleged contradiction, then there is no real contradiction. Books have been written to refute the alleged contradiction.

Sometimes the subtle attack on God's word is a semantic one. The assault way comes in language that asserts, "God talks God talk and we talk man talk." What these people fail to appreciate is the nature of revelation. Both old and new Testaments are given in **human language**. The Holy Spirit even used the vocabularies of the writers in the revelation of God's truth (II Pet 1:20,21; I Cor. 2:9-14).

The semantic attack may come through the questioning of the reliability of a translation from one language into another. "We don't have the original of a translation from one language into another. "We don't have the original autographs. All we have is a translation. It is difficult to translate one language into another language." It is difficult to translate one language into another, but not impossible. If it is impossible then international conferences such as the United Nations, and relations between foreign government would be impossible.

Furthermore, the study of important ancient books, such as *Plato's Republic,* would not be possible for those who rely on a translation from the original writing.

If Satan can use people to create doubt that we really have access to God's word, or that God really means what He has said in His word, then Satan's "fiery dart" has found its target.

Does God leave us defenseless in the struggle with Satan? No, we can take "the shield of faith" (Eph. 6:16). We can read what God has said and understand that word from God (Eph. 3:1-6; 5:17). We can trust God and commit our lives to Him.

Another "fiery dart" of the devil is ***discouragement***. One may, at a given time, have the courage to stand and withstand the schemes of Satan and yet that person can be beset with circumstances of life which so discourage him that he questions God's love, His power, His goodness, even His concern for the welfare of people, including His own children.

"Life is difficult," according to a prominent author and lecturer. In a sense though, M. Scott Peck, M. D., is echoing what a suffering man had said centuries ago: "Man who is born of woman is of few days and full of trouble" (Job 14:1).

One of Satan's effective schemes is to get people to blame God for Satan's destructive work. For example, in April, 1999, two students in a Colorado High School, one 18 years old and the other 17, went on a killing rampage. They used guns and pipe bombs to murder fellow students and one teacher. Then they allegedly killed themselves.

According to a report in USA Today, Monday, April 26, 1999, "People's faith is tested through this." The report states that on the marquee in front of a small nondenominational church the following question was posted: "Where was God Tuesday?" These people probably meant well; however, the wrong question was being asked.

The proper question was: "How did Satan do this?"

Do you for one moment think that these young murderers were Godrespecting, God-loving young men? People who love God respect the lives of others. They try to help people, not hurt them. They seek to do good, not evil.

Often, well-meaning people in their desire to comfort others will say to grieving people, "God took her." Or, "God took him." The hard truth is: He or she was a victim of Satan who has been murdering people since the dawn of time (John 8:44).

"But, why didn't God stop them? Where was God?" Why didn't God stop World War I and II before all of the death and misery had engulfed mankind? What about the Korean war and the horror of Vietnam?

Satan is the sinister force behind "man's inhumanity to man." People choose to be Satan's servants. God does not force His way of truth, peace and love on the human family. He did not create puppets to be manipulated.

However, the devil's destruction is decreed. His day is coming. He faces an eternal payday! (Rev. 20:10).

There is a time and there is a place where hate, misery, pain, destruction and death will be total strangers. An eternal kingdom where love, peace, and joy shall abound forever (Rev. 21:1-7).

Physical illness, the death of a loved one, family trouble, church troubles, are among a list of potential powers to discourage. However, God's promise is sure to His children: "The Lord is my helper, I will not fear what man shall do unto me" (Heb. 14:6, quoted from Psalms 118:6, ASV).

If people ever realize that Satan is the source of human misery and woe (I Pet. 5:8,9), maybe they will begin to resent, despise and rebel against him. Then, devil worship, the occult, and all false religions will loose their power to deceive and destroy people.

Another "fiery dart" of the devil is the ***doctrines of men*** (Col. 2:22). For ages the doctrines of men have been keeping people from the commandments of God.

The doctrines of men may come in the form of false philosophy (Col. 2:8). The doctrines may come in the distortion of God's truth (Col. 2:14-16). The false doctrines may come from the pride of mysticism which today proudly marches under the banner of a "new age religion."

The doctrines of men may emphasize one aspect of God's truth to the minimizing or distorting of equally necessary truth from God. For example, faith essential to please God (Heb. 11:6), and necessary to bring salvation through the Son of God (John 8:24; 20:30,31), may be emphasized to the minimizing of obedience to the gospel of Christ (Rom. 1:16,17; Heb. 5:8,9). Or, God's grace may be declared to the degree that obedience to God is either minimized or rejected altogether as being necessary to salvation (Acts 10:34,35). The doctrines of men can become walls of prejudice which keep people from knowing the truth of the Lord (John 8:32; 17:17).

Doctrines of a so-called "Social Gospel", and/or a "New Morality" may reject God's purpose, moral and ethical guidelines for His chosen and called people (Tit. 2:11-14).

The doctrine of a direct operation or working of the Holy Spirit separate and apart from the word of God can lead people into the sea of subjectivism and that sea has no distinct shoreline, and/or it can cause people to become victims to various false prophets and teachers who may claim, "God told me this", or "The Spirit revealed this to me."

It is ironic that some religious leaders will use the Bible to "prove" that the Bible is inadequate, that one must have a special leading of the

Holy Spirit. However, if the Spirit-directed revelation, the God-breathed Scripture (II Tim. 3:16, 17), furnishes us completely unto every good work then why is something in addition to that word necessitated?

Some rather serious charges have been made against the Bible by religious people who had accepted some authority in religion, in addition to the word of God and it is so sad to observe that when religious people accept an authority in addition to the Bible, it seems to become an authority other than the Bible.

Another "fiery dart" of Satan is ***deceptive pleasure.*** The excitement, the potential satisfaction, the immediate gratification of sin can so blind the mind to sin's consequences that one imagines he/she can reject God's restrictive commands and can reject with impunity (Ecc. 8:11).

While enjoying sin's pleasure, it is easy to forget the inevitable payday someday (Rom. 6:23).

Whatever the device, plot, or scheme he may use, Satan seeks to "numb the conscience, confuse the senses and paralyze the will" (Rogers and Rogers 504).

When He identified with humanity by becoming flesh and dwelling among us (John 1:14), Jesus faced the temptations of Satan (Matt. 4:1-11), however, Jesus was not deceived into doubting God's word. He withstood each temptation with God's word. "It is written," He declared.

Through a knowledge of Satan's reality, his personality, his plots and plans, and by taking God's whole or complete armor, we may indeed stand and withstand with courage born of faith, with dedication nurtured by a love for God, and with a hope built on a solid foundation of faith, we shall overcome the efforts of Satan and the victory will be to our eternal joy and to the glory of our God.

WORKS CITED

Foster, R.C. Studies In The Life of Christ. Grand Rapids: Baker Book House, 1971. Reprint.

Lenski, R.C.H. Commentary On The New Testament. Peabody, Mass: Hendrickson Publishers. 1998

McClintock, John. Cyclopedia of Biblical, Theological, and Ecclestiastical Literature. Grand Rapids: Baker Book House. Reprint. 1981.

Rogers, Cleon, Jr. and Cleon Rogers. The New Linguistic and Exegetical Key To The Greek New Testament. Grand Rapids: Condervan Pub. House. 1998.

Woods, Guy N. A Commentary on the New Testament. Nashville: Gospel Advocate Company. 1984.

Chapter 3

Satanism

Dan Wheeler

Do you know any Satanists? Since the early 1980's it has been claimed that some of our most trusted citizens—school teachers, judges, even ministers—are secret Devil worshippers who kidnap 400,000 victims each year. How much truth is there to this claim? Should we be fearful for the safety of our children as they walk down the street?

It is vital that we educate ourselves on the subject of Satanism—if we remain ignorant and fearful we cannot dispel the darkness of this religion from Hell. To understand Satanism, we will investigate the people involved, the book they call their Bible and the threat of this movement to us and to our children. You will see the absurdity of Satanism's dogma and the futility of its practices.

TYPES OF SATANISTS

The term "Satanist" is loosely applied to a variety of behaviors and beliefs, ranging from the serious practitioner to the obnoxious pretender. Such a loose application can be confusing. In order to separate fact from fiction it is useful to distinguish between *Religious Satanists* (Anton LaVey's Church of Satan), *Gothic Satanists* (a myth), *Satanic Dabblers* (experimenting adolescents) and *Quasi-Satanists* (pretenders).

Religious Satanism consists of three denominations: the Church of Satan, the Temple of Set, and the Church of Satanic Liberation. Contrary to popular perception these groups are not Devil worshippers;

in fact, they do not even believe in the Devil! "Satan" is their term for the force of nature that represents power and sexuality and is derived from the ancient Egyptian deity Set. Religious Satanists consider the Devil to be a Christian myth. They rebel against religion, calling it the "spiritual status quo." Individually they can be characterized as eccentric but peaceful adults who are serious about their Satanic belief. Collectively, the number of religious Satanists in North America is unknown because the largest group (the Church of Satan) does not release its membership totals. A U.S. Army pamphlet in the late 1970's alleged that there are 10 to 20 thousand Satanists. Surely this number is inflated, if the1991 Canadian census is any indication: only 335 Canadians identified themselves as Satanists!

Although many of us equate Satanism with Devil-worshipping, soul-selling cults who commit unspeakable acts of horror, religious tolerance advocates claim that these horrific activities are largely a figment of the public imagination. They call this stereotype *Gothic Satanism* and claim it is merely a myth created by church leaders in Medieval times. They admit that there may be a few Devil worshippers today but deny that they commit crimes or hurt other people.

Satanic Dabblers are usually adolescent males who like to disturb others and rebel against authority. They become engrossed in occult books, heavy metal music, and Satanic symbols. Dabblers often mix elements of Religious Satanism, Medieval Satanism and magic into their secret ceremonies, so the rituals may involve candles, small animal sacrifices, drug use and/or sexual conduct (Wheeler, Wood, and Hatch, 1988, in Otten and Myers, p. 68-69). Dabblers occasionally commit minor yet alarming crimes such as cemetery vandalism and Satanic graffiti. There are presumably thousands of young people involved at any given time, but accurate numbers are elusive since there is no central organization and involvement does not last for a long period of time.

Ostentatious Satanists range from teenagers to rock musicians to criminals, and have at least one thing in common: they are not serious about their newly found "faith" but they enjoy the resulting attention. In some communities, teenage "Goths" (not to be confused with *Gothic Satanism*) roam the malls wearing ghoulish white makeup and dressed in black. Professional musicians also get in on the act. The last quarter of the twentieth century saw an explosion in the number of supposed Satanists in the rock music industry. Heavy metal groups such as K.I.S.S., Black Sabbath, Ozzy Ozborn and Marilyn Manson pretended to be Satanists to gain publicity. This did wonders for their concert attendance and record sales. In addition to the musicians, serious criminals (arsonists, child molesters and serial killers) use Satanism to either excuse their activities or intimidate the public. For example, an arson suspect arrested after a series of nationwide church fires told reporters that Satan told him to commit the crimes. The most infamous criminal/Satanist of all, convicted murderer Charles Manson, created a wave of fear during his 1970 serial murder trial when he glared at jurors for hours and yelled "Hail Satan!" as he was removed from the courtroom. Public fear has since insured Manson's repeated denial of parole from his life sentence.

FOUNDERS OF RELIGIOUS SATANISM

Despite the claim that religious Satanism is an ancient tradition there are two modern names who gave the Satanic movement its notoriety: Aleister Crowley and Anton LaVey. Both of these men had a knack for publicity that served to win followers and propagate their views.

Crowley (1875-1947) was raised in a Plymouth Brethren family but rebelled against religion early. He adopted a perversion of the Golden Rule: do what you want to do. After college he joined the Order of the Golden Dawn and became a well-known magician. His secret occult society reportedly ousted him for homosexuality, drug abuse, and murder. Later, he made outlandish claims—that he was the Beast of Revelation, that he had the ability to become invisible, and that he possessed the fountain of youth. Although defenders of Crowley attribute his bizarre reputation to tabloid journalism, they admit that he encouraged such stories for the sake of publicity.

Anton Szandor LaVey (1930-1997) was a charismatic man of varied experiences: he was an accomplished professional musician, a police photographer, and a circus worker. He drew from his study of psychology and magic to write the Satanic Bible (1969), The Compleat Witch (1970) and The Satanic Rituals (1972). He founded the Church of Satan in 1966 on April 30th (six months from Halloween) and proclaimed it the Satanic holiday of Walpurgisnacht.

The Satanic movement split in 1975 when Michael Aquino left the Church of Satan to form the Temple of Set (ToS). Although Aquino agreed with LaVey's doctrine, he felt that LaVey's recent reorganization of the Church of Satan had been selfish and greedy. Aquino resigned from the church in protest, claiming that the true ideals of Satanism had been lost, and led defectors to form the new group. Two entities dominate ToS literature and websites: the depiction of the Egyptian god Set as a man with the head of an animal, and the buzzword "Xeper" (pronounced "Khefer"). Xeper is a coined word that Setians say means "I am come to be." It is the process of self-actualization, achieved through the individual's pursuit of a variety of interests. Xeper is inhibited by drug use, which is therefore discouraged by the Temple of Set.

THE DOCTRINE OF RELIGIOUS SATANISM

"Religious" Satanism is a misnomer—these Satanists do not believe in God, Heaven, Hell, or even the Devil. It is more accurate to describe their movement as a humanistic, Epicurean philosophy. It is the worship of self-indulgence, and it uses "Satan"—a force of nature—to further the goals of the individual. Its dogma reflects a disdain for religion (the Black Mass is a parody of the Catholic church). LaVey prescribed ceremonies, a code of conduct, and the Nine Satanic statements for the Church of Satan.

Church of Satan rituals are elaborate, eccentric, and erotic. The altar is a trapezoidal table placed against the west wall (originally, LeVey used a nude woman as the altar). Black predominates a Satanic ceremony: black candles represent the powers of darkness; males wear long black robes and young women wear sexually suggestive black clothing. At the beginning and end of the ritual, the priest rings a bell while rotating counter-clockwise. On a small table next to the altar is placed a chalice made of silver. Gold is avoided because Wiccans use it, and Religious Satanist detest being associated with the Wiccans. The ritual is performed in Enochian, an ancient language that sounds similar to Hebrew, Latin or Arabic. Satanists use three types of magic rituals: sex magic; a healing/happiness ritual; and a destruction ritual (consisting of sticking pins in a doll or drawing pictures of the victim's death).

The Church of Satan's code of conduct is a silly attempt to mock Christianity. Prayer, a vital part of the Christian faith (1 Thess. 5:17), is ridiculed as useless and distracting. Satanists are taught not to turn the other cheek, but to retaliate immediately ("smash him on the other"). LaVey's Bible smugly instructs the Satanist to relish the "seven deadly sins" (greed, pride, envy, anger, gluttony, lust and sloth). It encourages sexual behavior (heterosexuality, homosexuality and bisexuality). Ironically, the final rule of behavior is that the Satanist needs no formal rule of behavior!

Anton LaVey wrote the Nine Satanic Statements; they are decidedly sarcastic and anti-religious. The statements claim that Satan represents the following concepts: 1) indulgence, not abstinence; 2) vital existence, not spiritual pipe dreams; 3) undefiled wisdom, not hypocritical self-deceit; 4) kindness to those deserving of it, not love wasted on ingrates; 5) vengeance, not turning the other cheek; 6) responsibility to the responsible, instead of concern for psychic vampires; 7) man as just another animal—the most vicious of all (due to spiritual development); 8) all of the so-called sins, as they all lead to physical, mental, or emotional gratification; 9) the best friend the Church has ever had as he has kept it in business all these years.

ASSUMPTIONS OF THE SATANIC BIBLE

The Satanic Bible (LaVey, 1969) consists of three parts: an attack on mainstream religion, a defense of Satanism, and a collection of Satanic rituals for the reader to control the world around him. The rhetoric of the Satanic Bible is not the work of a genius, for it is full of false assumptions and faulty logic.

First of all, the Satanic Bible assumes that having fun and being religious are mutually exclusive. LaVey misrepresents Christianity as an undesirable, deprived lifestyle and then labels pleasure as "Satanic." This portrayal is false because God's Word does not prohibit Christians from pleasure (in its proper place). A stoic lifestyle ("taste not, touch not, handle not") is useless (Colossians 2:20-22). However, the Bible warns us that a life without restraint (a Satanic lifestyle) will lead to depression and despair. Solomon discovered this firsthand and wrote the Book of Ecclesiastes to show this from his own experience (Ecclesiastes 2:10-11).

The Satanic Bible assumes that humans are inherently violent and concludes that turning the other cheek is an act of weakness. This assertion is simply LaVey's attempt to justify his juvenile notion about vengeance ("If your enemy strikes you on one cheek, smash him on the other."). This assumption denies the fact that it takes maturity, self-control and strength to be a peacemaker. Jesus, our greatest example, was not weak. Physically, He was strong enough to perform the laborious work of a carpenter and spend long hours with the masses of people in need. Emotionally, He was strong enough to endure sorrow, disappointment and rejection. Spiritually, He was strong enough to avoid sin, resist the Devil's temptations and avoid calling on angels to deliver Him from the horror of the cross. The example of the Prince of Peace shows that violence is not a solution to problems, nor is it an indication of strength; it does not result in the righteousness of God (James 1:19-20).

LaVey's disdain of religion is behind a third assumption of his bible: religion is bad and anything antagonistic to it ("evil") must be beneficial. This twisted logic works as a widening wedge between adolescents and their religious parents who condemn their Satanic association. The Devil tried to reverse the concepts of good and evil in the garden of Eden (Genesis 3:1-6). He is responsible for society portraying evil behavior in a positive light (fornication is a "relationship;" abortion is "planned parenthood," and homosexuality is "cultural diversity"). The Devil maligns Christian morality as "Victorian," "patriarchal," "homophobic," or countless other epithets. The prophet Isaiah warned us long ago, "Woe unto them that call evil good, and good evil; that put darkness for light, and light for darkness; that put bitter for sweet, and sweet for bitter" (Isaiah 5:20).

The Satanic Bible assumes that enemies can be conquered through Satanic power. This rhetoric plays on the insecurities of the adolescent who has personal conflicts (Moriarty, 1992). The reader is lead to see intimidation as a way of gaining respect from his enemies (this includes anyone opposed to his Satanic involvement). This approach to conflict resolution is irresponsible: it ignores the pitfalls of elevating conflict. Jesus' words have become an accepted maxim, "Those that live by the sword shall die by the sword" (Matthew 26:52). Christianity has a better approach to taking care of enemies: kindness. Returning good for evil is as effective in neutralizing an enemy as "heaping coals of fire on his head (Romans 12:20). After the best way to destroy an enemy is to make him a friend.

LaVey chides Christians as "gazers beyond the grave" and argues that Satanism is the only religion relevant to modern life. This assumption reveals LaVey's prejudice toward the Word of God—he denies that the Bible has sustained many people through the most trying times of their lives. The Bible deals with many earthly matters such as work, health, friendships, citizenship, dealing with enemies, how to treat the poor, home life, and even sexual fulfillment. Living a godly life and following God's way has relevance to not only eternal life but to the here and now (1 Timothy 4:8). In other words, God's Word teaches us how to live on earth so that we can live with Him in Heaven.

The promise of power is common to all occult philosophies and is enticing to those who feel helpless (Moriarty, 1992). The Satanic Bible assumes that the Enochian Keys—a long list of rambling prayers—provides the Satanist with power to get what he wants. The belief in the Keys is contradictory to the fact that Satanists are athiests who do not believe in prayer! The vanity of chanting ancient prayers to an inanimate universe is in stark contrast to the comforting promises of

Christianity. The righteous are seen and heard by the Lord (1 Peter 3:12). Also, Ephesians 3:20 promises that God can do above all that we ask or think. While God once worked miracles until His revelation was completed in the first century (see 1 Corinthians 13:10), He now provides for us through His providence and care. The Christian knows that "all things work together for good" for those that love God (Romans 8:28). Truly it is the Christian who has the Power of the Universe ready to aid him in matters of "life and godliness" (2 Peter 1:3).

Like Madison Avenue, LaVey learned that sex sells. Therefore, another assumption of the Satanic Bible is that Satanism offers sexual paradise while Christianity prohibits it. Many adolescents struggle with sexuality and are vulnerable to this lie. To protect them parents must teach them that sexuality is a holy creation that is not to be misused. The Bible says that marriage is "honorable" and the "bed" is "undefiled: but whoremongers and adulterers God will judge" (Hebrews 13:4). Sexual pleasure is not forbidden to the Christian. In fact, husbands and wives are encouraged to "render due benevolence" to each other (1 Corinthians 7:3). Solomon advises husbands to "rejoice with the wife of your youth" (Proverbs 6:18). While the Satanist is taught to get gratification by any legal or practical means, the Christian is taught that true fulfillment can only be found in the security of a scriptural marriage (1 Corinthians 7:2). The only way to practice "safe sex" is to wear a wedding ring.

In summary, the warped rhetoric of the Satanic Bible is based upon assumptions that are easily refuted. Common sense and even a cursory amount of Bible knowledge will help the Christian to easily see through this nonsense. God's people have no reason to be intimidated by this idiotic philosophy. Our disgust of the Satanic Bible will make us treasure the words of Jesus, "And you shall know the truth, and the truth shall make you free" (John 8:32). Never have the words of Jesus been more relevant than in the battle for young souls.

PERSONALITY TYPES OF SATANIC DABBLERS

Some young Satanists are extremely self-confident and they attribute this to Satanism's mind-altering power. However, personality traits are likely to be the cause rather than the result of Satanic involvement. In fact, experts view dabbling as a sign of previously existing emotional problems (TerHorst, 1988, in Otten and Myers, p. 70). Moriarty (1992) describes teenage dabblers in terms of four disturbed personality types: the *psychopathic delinquent,* the *angry misfit,* the *pseudo-intellectual*, and the *suicidal impulsive.* Each type has its own motivational factors, emotional benefit derived from involvement, and intervention strategy.

The *psychopathic delinquent* is as dangerous as the term implies. He (this type is almost always male) is cruel, abusive and enjoys degrading others. Satanism is not so much a religion for him as it is an excuse for committing crime and possessing dangerous weapons. This type of dabbler is highly resistant to counseling, so change is unlikely. The focus of intervention must be on public safety. The most effective way to curb the threat of the psychopathic delinquent is through arrest and prosecution.

The *angry misfit* is less hostile than the delinquent. His anger is repressed and he is vicariously involved in violence through movies or music. However, he grows angrier without the aggressive beat of heavy metal music. The angry misfit is argumentative and irrationally blames others for his own actions—behavior that indicates distress and a cry for help. The best intervention strategy is counseling; meanwhile, parents of an angry misfit should try to remain calm during this time of turmoil.

The *pseudo-intellectual* is the least aggressive of the dabblers types. He or she gets great satisfaction from his knowledge of the occult and enjoys mental domination of others. His knowledge produces a superiority complex and the belief that he is resistant to intervention. Ironically, the pseudo-intellectual is a victim of faulty critical thinking. He accepts a Satanic book or website on face value. The best intervention strategy is not to attack his beliefs directly but to challenge the way this dabbler discovers truth. For example, to encourage him to think critically, he should be asked why he thinks Anton LaVey, an atheist, prescribed the Black Mass, a "religious" ritual. Hopefully the dabbler will realize that the Church of Satan is not a religion, but a parody against religion.

The *suicidal impulsive* may be the most disturbed type of dabbler. This type of adolescent feels a lack of control over his environment, so toying with the possibility of suicide helps him regain control over his/her own life. His obsession with death causes him to be extremely reckless. Satanic rituals provide a way to justify the suicidal tendencies. The best intervention for a suicidal impulsive is decisive: hospitalization and separation from Satanist companions.

In sum, many young Satanic dabblers have emotional problems that lead to their Satanic involvement. These pre-existing problems must be addressed if Satanic involvement is to be terminated.

THE INFLUENCE OF PARENTS

Attributing Satanic involvement to emotional or mental problems does not absolve parents from their parenting responsibility, for many of these problems are caused by controllable external factors. Unstable family life, media influence and peer pressure can all impact the healthy development of children. Parents can eliminate or soften the destructiveness of these factors by following the suggestions below.

Marriage must be held in higher regard. Divorce is too common. Most children of divorce are emotionally injured and spiritually neglected. They have been traumatized by the fracture of their home. They are often unsupervised during the day and are susceptible to getting into trouble. No wonder some Juvenile law enforcement officials place today's youth problems squarely on the prevalence of divorce in our culture. Parents should be proactive by working on the marriage to stay together rather than bail out because of marital trouble.

Television viewing must be kept to a minimum. Relatively few television shows don't contain sexual innuendoes, sexual situations, gratuitous violence or increasingly blasphemous situations. Watch television with the remote control handy so that the volume can be muted during commercials. Take a stand against sin by turning the channel or turning off the television. The innocence of children is slowly taken away by the often sacrilegious one-eyed baby-sitter.

Computer use must be controlled. Parents should severely limit or deny access to chatrooms because of the prevalence of bad language. Use an Internet provider that filters out offensive material. Keep the computer in an open area of the house where parents can monitor the monitor! Over one-half of the millions of websites contain "adult content." Giving a child unlimited access to the Internet in the privacy of his/her room invites trouble.

Know your child's friends. Have them over where they can be supervised. Most adolescents seek approval from their peers and gravitate toward some kind of club or groups. Even criminal or Satanic rings are enticing to those desperate for acceptance. Parents should discourage friendships with those who are a bad influence on their child.

Family devotionals should be a regular part of family life. The family that prays together stays together. Christian fathers should take the lead in this and see that his family daily communes with God together. The bonds created early between parents and children in a Christian home will pay eternal dividends. It is not likely that a child raised in a godly home will turn suddenly from the truth to his own spiritual destruction. The wise man wrote, "Train up a child in the way he should go: and when he is old, he will not depart from it" (Proverbs 22:6). Now more than ever we need parents who will take this proverb to heart.

INDICATIONS OF SATANIC INVOLVEMENT

Parents trying to assess their children's satanic involvement may look for obvious clues (i.e., Satanic symbols such as pentagrams, the baphomet, and religious words spelled backwards), but subtle indicators should not be ignored. For example, frequent respiratory problems can be triggered by illegal drugs—a staple of Satanic cults. In addition, sudden recovery from emotional problems may be due to Satanic involvement or even plans for suicide. Furthermore, the emergence of friends who remain unknown to the parents may indicate some covert activity (Moriarty, 1992). Parents who are oblivious to these physical, psychological, and social indicators provide ample opportunity for their children to become entangled in the Satanic mire.

THE REAL DANGER OF SATANISM

Is Satanism a real threat, or is it just a harmless fad? An accurate answer requires consideration of the issue from physical, mental, and spiritual aspects.

The claim that secret Satanic cults are widespread and kidnap 400,000 people a year is attributed to Michelle Remembers, a 1980 book revealing victim Michelle Smith's memories of Satanic ritual abuse. No one has been able to substantiate its claims, but the urban legend of a dangerous conspiracy persists to this day. In order to verify this claim that there is no threat to the public safety, the author turned to local law enforcement agencies (one in Fort Worth, Texas, where the author was speaking on the subject, and several in Central Florida, where the author lives). Inquiries consistently brought the same result: law enforcement agencies consider Satanic cults to be only a minor nuisance. One Central Florida Sheriff's deputy admits that his main job is public relations—keeping down the Satanic panic that occasionally resurfaces whenever the media reports a crime as having a cult connection.

Now consider whether Satanism is a danger to one's mental health. Despite the impression one gets from Hollywood movies, Satanism has no supernatural mind-controlling power. Satanists cannot cast spells and turn victims into zombies. Satanism is merely a selfish, atheistic philosophy. Its doctrine is based on faulty assumptions, weak logic, and adolescent appeal. The healthy mind has nothing to fear. Christians can easily refute Satanism and must not be intimidated by it.

FINALLY, CONSIDER THE SPIRITUAL DANGER OF SATANISM

Since true Satanists are not Devil worshippers, can it be concluded that the Satanic movement is harmless to the soul? Hardly! The chants, pentagrams, black shrouds and candles are a parody of religion and a rejection of God. Satanism is more scornful of Christianity than any other philosophy. God hates such rebellion (Proverbs 6:16,17) as well as involvement with the occult (1 Samuel 15:23). Those that do not love the truth of God's Word will not be saved (2 Thessalonians 2:10). Those that do not believe will be damned (Mark 16:16). Those who do not obey God have no hope (Ephesians 2:12). Therefore, Satanists who do not repent will be miserable in Hell for eternity, a condition that they do not now take seriously.

One day every proud proponent of Hell will tremble before the throne of Heaven: "For it is written, As I live, saith the Lord, every knee shall bow to me, and every tongue shall confess to God" (Romans 14:11). Each one of us will "confess that Jesus Christ is Lord, to the glory of God the Father" (Philippians 2:10-11). However, the worship of God at the Judgment Day will be too late to save the Satanist's soul from dreadful damnation. Considering that Hell is a place of eternal misery, darkness, torment and despair, each Satanist should seriously ask himself, "What in Hell do I want?" and then soberly realize, "Nothing!"

WORKS CITED

Hicks, R.D. (1991). "The Police Model of Satanic Crime." The Satanic Scare, ed. Bromley, D. G. Best, J., and Richardson, J. T. New York: Aldine de Gruyter, 1991.

Kahaner, L. Cults that Kill. New York: Warner Books, 1988.

LaVey, A. The Satanic Bible. New York: Avon Press, 1969.

Moriarty, A. The Psychology of Adolescent Satanism. Westport, CT: Praeger, 1992.

Meade, J. "Satanism." Teacher Magazine, September/October 1991.

Ottens, A. J. and Myer, R. Coping with Satanism. New York: Rosen Publishing Group, 1994.

Simandl, R. J. and Maysmith, B. "Dabbling their Way to Ritual Crime." Cult Awareness News, August 1988.

Smith, Michelle. Michelle Remembers. New York: Congdon & Lattes, 1980.

TerHorst, C. "The Dark Side of Adolescence." Palestine (IL) Daily Herald, 1988.

Wheeler, B. R., Wood, S. and Hatch, R. J. "Assessing and Intervention with Adolescents Involved in Satanism." Social Work (November-December, 1988).

Http://swampwitch.com/pegged.html

Http://cit.itc.virginia.edu/~jkh8x/soc257/nrms/satanism/pop.html

Chapter 4

Black Magic

Darrell Conley

INTRODUCTION

Ever since I was a small boy (I am now in my sixtieth year), my hobby has been magic; not black magic, but sleight of hand, the kind of magic that attempts to entertain people by performing that which seems magical. I have learned that among magicians there are both those who are honest deceivers and those who are dishonest deceivers. That is, there are those who readily admit and even insist that what they are doing are simply tricks. They are fooling people for the sake of entertainment. And there are those who claim to actually be performing supernatural feats, usually some kind of psychic phenomena. Martin Gardner, who was for years the writer of the scientific amusements column for *The Scientific American* magazine, and who is an accomplished magician with a number of magic books to his credit, says:

> "The purpose of conjuring, at least most of the time, is to entertain audiences by pretending to violate natural laws . . . The magician . . . is a consumate liar. His principles, borrowed in part from physics and psychology . . ., are soaked through and through with deliberate falsification of the most reprehensible sort. It is not so much what a magician says as what he implies. He will show the queen of hearts, turn it face down on top of the deck, and apparently deal it the table. He may even say, "And well place the queen over here," knowing full well the card he is

> putting there is no longer the queen. But most of the time it is what the magician does, not what he says, that is deceptive. He may tap an object to prove it solid when only the spot he taps is solid. He may casually show the palm of his hand to prove he has nothing concealed when something is on the back of his hand" (Gardner 91-92).

The difference, then, between the honest magician and the dishonest magician is not one of deception. Both deceive. But one admits he is deceiving and the other does not.

In this chapter I plan to deal with the latter kind of magic--black magic. By "black magic" I mean magic that is done to seriously deceive or magical ritual done with evil intent whether believed in or not. Some of those who are involved in the weirder aspects of black magic and the occult are believers themselves as well as practitioners. We will deal with both kinds of "black magic": those who deceive the public by various means, and those who are themselves deceived and involved in the evil and wickedness of "black magic."

FRADULENT MAGIC

Artur Zorka

Only recently I was browsing the Internet and ran across a web-page run by Mike Hutchinson. He is a humanist, but an anti-occultist, so I read what he had to say. Among the articles he had written, I ran across a name I recognized--Artur Zorka. He referred to Zorka's authentication of the claimed psychic Uri Geller in Atlanta, Georgia, back in the 1970's. I immediately e-mailed Mike what information I had which started the exchange of several messages and eventually of books each of us had written. This is what I told him.

Artur Zorka's real name is Art Glick. He was a member of the Atlanta Society of Magicians. I knew him well. I was in my second term as president of that club at the time I moved to New Orleans. As president I formed the Occult Investigations Committee of that local society and appointed Art Glick, Abb Dixon, myself, and perhaps others to it. We never investigated anybody. After I moved away, I got a call from the president of the national Society of American Magicians wanting to know what about this group that had met with and authenticated Uri Geller. He was especially outraged because the national society had an occult investigations committee and he thought they were claiming to be it. Although I explained to him how that committee had begun, I also told him that they had no right or authority to speak for anybody or to authenticate anyone. I also told him that Glick was a pretended psychic himself. This was the kind of magic that he specialized in. He also had shown himself in an incident, in the Governor Carter's office, to be hungry for publicity. I also have a newspaper clipping that has a picture in it that shows him being arrested and handcuffed for driving blindfolded through the streets of Decatur, Georgia, as a publicity stunt without first obtaining a permit from the police department. His authentication of Geller was evidently just another effort at publicity and amounted to nothing.

Neither can one put one's faith in Abb Dixon. Although he was later elected president of the International Brotherhood of Magicians, his tenure in office was marred when he was arrested and pled guilty to a crime in Georgia.

WHO ARE IN THE BEST POSITION TO TEST THE CLAIMS OF THE OCCULT?

Magicians, if they are honest themselves (and competent), are in the best position to test those who claim to do real magic. They are familiar with the many methods of deceit that are commonly used and, therefore, are less likely to be fooled. On the contrary, scientists, who often test psychics, are not the best qualified to do so.

> "Any magician will tell you that scientists are the easiest persons in the world to fool. It is not hard to understand why. In their laboratories the equipment is just what it seems. There are no hidden mirrors or secret compartments or concealed magnets. If an assistant puts chemical A in a beaker he doesn't (usually) surreptitiously switch it for chemical B. The thinking of a scientist is rational, based on a lifetime of experience with a rational world. But the methods of magic are irrational and totally outside a scientist's experience. The general public has never understood this. Most people assume that if a man has a brilliant mind he is qualified to detect fraud. This is untrue. Unless he has been thoroughly trained in the underground art of magic, and knows its peculiar principles, he is easier to deceive than a child" (Gardner 92).

Gardner points out that whereas a magician must perform what he has promised to, a "psychic" like Geller need not, if he feels the 'vibes" are not right, or if he comes up with some other excuse. He states at the very beginning that he doesn't know whether anything will happen or not, so he is certainly not to be blamed if nothing does. Skeptics are thereby disarmed.

For instance, in bending keys Gardner points out how Geller waits until everyone's attention is elsewhere (called "misdirection" in magic--sometimes with Geller this takes thirty minutes or more), and then he bends the key, with his strong fingers, against a table, or chair, or whatever is handy, hides it, perhaps, among other keys, and goes back to it later and pretends to bend it by gently stroking it. He often obtains his misdirection by rushing from one thing to another, creating chaos. Geller is a run-of-the-mill magician, not a true psychic.

WHAT ABOUT ESP?

One of the few forms of entertainment magic that many people are still willing to believe are genuine is what magicians call mentalism--fake ESP. (Is there any other kind?) Those magicians who allow people to believe they can actually read minds or claim to have supernormal powers are frauds. I have conducted workshops in Houston, Corpus Christi, Austin, and San Antonio exposing the occult for what it is.

Extra-Sensory Perception falls into four categories: 1) Telepathy--the ability to know what is in another person's mind without the normal senses; 2) Clairvoyance--the knowledge of a thing or happening obtained without using the usual means of communication; 3) Precognition--knowing ahead of time what is going to happen; 4) Psychokinesis--the ability to cause an object to move by using the mind alone.

The major ESP experiments and their outcomes have been: 1) The Rhine experiments of the 1930's. They are now generally admitted to have been poorly designed and allowed the communication of information between subject and tester. 2) The SRI remote-viewing experiments of the 1970's of Harold Putoff and Russell Targ. The National Research Council says: "By both scientific and parapsychological standards, then, the case for remote viewing is not just very weak, but virtually nonexistent." 3) Research on random-number generators. The National Research Council reports that "after 15 years of research, only one of hundreds of experiments met the minimal criteria of scientific acceptability, and that one experiment yielded results of just marginal significance." 4) The Ganzfield experiment. These are probably the most carefully conducted and scrutinized ESP experiments. "Still, the research has failed to produce results that convince psychologists that ESP exists. In summary, the existence of ESP has not been demonstrated in either everyday life or the laboratory" ("utdallas").

Anyone who claims to be able to foresee the future through pyschic means is fraudulent. They are deceiving you for money, publicity or fun. When I was in New Orleans a young man who was a member of the Society of American Magicians came to the monthly meeting and related one of the things that sometimes occur. He was entertaining at an event and in one trick pretended to predict a newspaper headline. It so happened that the newspaper headline he predicted was the collision of the two airliners in the Caribbean that killed so many people. He made such an impression on the people with that trick, that his (pretended) prediction was reported in the newspaper itself. The next thing he knew, he had been invited to appear on the Tonight Show with Johnny Carson. He asked us what he should do. I responded that he should not go. He ought to admit it was a trick and excuse himself after considering this advice; that's what he did.

Unfortunately, many do not. Perhaps we remember the supposed "Top Psychic" James Hydrick, who was exposed as a fake by magician and occult investigator, James Randi. After making the pages of a book turn "psychically" in rehearsal, and hearing by means of a hidden microphone that he was secretly blowing over the pages of the book, Randi put pieces of styrofoam around the book during the actual performance that would be blown about by any breath of air. As a result he was unable to make the pages turn (Randi 16). He later admitted he used trickery.

Randi also exposed the fake predictions of Alan Vaughan. He offered Vaughn $10,000.00 if he could demonstrate under test conditions, by psychic means which often cans a ball bearing was in. In thirty-six different tests he found the ball bearing only three times.

Hardly a record that comports with the law of averages, much less with psychic ability! In forty-six newspaper predictions, Vaughn was totally wrong twenty-six times, right no times, so vague the outcome was not determinable fourteen times, and the outcome not yet determinable six times (Ibid 16).

This does not stop many from believing in psychic phenomena. In a poll taken several years ago among college students who had taken a course in which a magician had demonstrated how "psychics" fool people, the following figures were obtained: 86% believed in telepathy; 79% believed in precognition; 71% believed in clairvoyance; 64% believed in ghosts; 46% believed in astrology. In a Gallop poll taken the same year of the American people, the following figures in the same categories were obtained: 51% believed in telepathy; 37% believed in precognition; 24% believed in clairvoyance; 11% believed in ghosts; and 29% believed in astrology (Greenwell 44). Although the figures obtained by the Gallop poll are less, they are still too high.

OCCULTLIC MAGIC

What Is This Kind of Black Magic?

Black magic in the broadest sense covers most of the subjects included in this book. It is synonymous with "occult." Several years ago I authored a book on the occult which has recently been reprinted by Apologetics Press called The Gospel Versus Occultism. In it I addressed many of these topics. Although I will do my best not to intrude too deeply into the subject matter of the other writers, I will of necessity touch on some of the things they have been asked to write about.

Black magic is defined as "Magic used in the occult to bring evil, cursings, or negative effects on the person(s) to whom it is directed.

The witch, sorcerer, or magician conjures up evil spirits and invokes them to carry out the intended harm" (Mather & Nichols 40). The Magician's Dictionary contains this quotation: "One of the preoccupations of magic is to enlist gods, spirits, elementals, etc. to do one's bidding and to release their power to the practitioner. But the black magician seeks unlimited power, not to borrow, but to appropriate for himself not in order to better the world or himself, but to satisfy his personal greed and to establish his ambitious tyranny" (Dictionary).

There is a fascination with the evil and dark side of things. Although this has always been true, it has grown and spread tremendously in the last few years, especially among young, impressionable, and morally destitute young people. They have been taught that there is no God, that there is no absolute right or wrong, every thing is relative, the Bible is a book of myths, prayer has been outlawed in the public school, and we no longer live in a Christian nation or culture. They are, in too many instances, replacing good spiritual values with evil. Only think of the recent events in Littleton, Colorado, where two young men dressed all in black killed and injured numerous other young people and teachers at a school and then killed themselves. They were into the occult and boasted about the evil they believed in. They dressed and acted the part. Yet no one took them seriously. It seems that all that the news media wants to talk about is gun control. The evil goes much deeper than that. These young men were a reflection of the lack of morals in the music, movies, books, and television in our culture.

The magician (here I speak, not of the entertainer, nor of the one who uses trickery to deceive, but of one who is involved in the occult) is one who believes that the forces of nature can be controlled and manipulated by the application of certain formulas, rituals, and techniques. There have been such magicians as early as we have record. There were certainly magicians in various pagan religions. There were the magicians of Baal who failed in the contest with Elijah on Mt. Carmel. The Kabbala of the Jews is their occult tradition. The Middle Ages saw the production of such books of magic as The Grand Grimoire, The Grimotre of Honorieus, The Key of Solomon, and The Lessor Key of Solomon" (Freedland 158).

Aleister Crowley

The most famous of the twentieth century black magicians was Aleister Crowley, who called himself the Great Beast 666. Although he was raised in a family that belonged to the Plymouth Brethren and was a brewery heir with a great fortune, he soon left his religion and spent his life squandering his substantial inheritance. He was twenty-three years old when he was first initiated into the English magic society, the Order of the Golden Dawn, a group of knowledgeable occultists. Also members were William Butler Yeats and Algernon Blackwood. Crowley mostly destroyed the order when he tried to take it over and finally founded his own small group, the Argentinum Astrum.

He became known in the English press as "The Wickedest Man in the World." His Law of Thelema says, "This Book lays down a simple Code of Conduct. Do what thou wilt shall be whole of the Law. Love is the Law, love under will. There is no law beyond Do what thou wilt" (Larson 152). His disciples often went mad or died. Drugs were taken at his gatherings with abandon and animals were sacrificed in an effort to "raise the ancient gods." He maintained a harem that constantly changed, as well as engaging in homosexual acts. During World War I, he came to America to New York and put out pro-German propaganda which he later tried to excuse as satire when Germany lost the war.

He wrote a book that has been very influential in black magic circles called *Magick in Theory and Practice*. Crowley died in 1947 at the age of seventy-two. At the end he was a heroin addict, receiving eleven grams of heroin daily. This is not surprising in one who did not believe in God, right or wrong, heaven or hell, and had no real purpose for being. He died bankrupt, a drug-addict and mentally incompetent. But he remains a hero to the occultist of today and to many of the rock musicians, including Ozzie Ozborn and the Beatles.

The Evil on the Internet

The following are a few of the sites I have found on the Internet and brief self-descriptions of what they contain. I have tried to weed out those who are just playing, however poor their taste may be. Those that remain seem to be serious. What they have to offer is truly shocking (I am not giving references to where these sites can be found because I do not want to encourage anyone to patronize them, but I assure you, they are there). *Gaither Graphix*: "Fine art for the Criminally Insane." *The Satanic Kindrid*: "My views on ancient and La Vayan [sic] Satanism. . . . I also give out 10 different awards from most gruesome to most satanic!" *Cataleptic 666's Home Page*: "Come and see for yourself" *The Charles Manson Fun Page*!: "An irreverent look at the darker side of life!" *THE TEXAS TERROR*: "The Texas Chainsaw Massacre, Scream, Horror News and lots of Honor Links." *T.U.B.A.*: "Axemurder as a hobby." *A Bad Place*: "A site with links to all things dark and scary." *Pier for the Dead*: "This site was made so I could have the freedom to bring out my darker side. This site also gives the freedom to other people and encourages them to do the same." *The Halls of the Damned*: "The Halls of the Damned is the home of the Evil-Elf, a Satanist, an unholy missionary of the Antichrist and a [sic] all around Evil guy. This site is dedicated to Satanism and it also includes stuff on Anton La Vey, Marilyn Manson and lots more!

A huge library covering Satan to Lucifer and all the stuff in-between. Hail Satan, Hail Lucifer, Hail Belial, Hail Leviathan!" *Steiner's House of Pain*: "This is the place, where death joyfully hurries to life's aid...and you will experience the things people usually prefer no[t] to see, though they are all around us. Sadness and fear tortures us and we live in a big depression, as we have no belief neither [sic] in god not in satan as they both don't care about us little human.., and our doomed death cult in our insane existence." *The Shadowmantium*: "Shadowmantium: Abode of Darkness; Noctuary, Satanic Philosophy . . . Horror. . . Blasphemy, Rebellion, & Diabolic Links." *Reality's A Crutch*: "The one indestructible force, the one certain thing in an uncertain universe: DEATH." *Demonic Church of the Maridian Order*: "Visit the Demonic Church of the Maridian Order and read the Testimonies of the DEMON! Learn how to join with the Church." *KILL THE CHRISTIAN'S WEBRING*: "Help us bring about the downfall of the Christian faith. Submit articles to enlighten the masses." *The Executioness's Horror Dungeon*: "A honor site with everything and more! Have you hugged your serial killer today?" *Evil Minds*: "Evil creativity from the evil minds of the world." *D's domain*: "Just hoping to make it in this dark world, when my only friend seems to be the darkness." *Trendkillers Darkside*: "All that is dark & evil." *Derelict of Damnation*: "Dark poetry of both mine and visitors. No Christians allowed!"

The quotes above (and many more) are almost enough to make one believe that we are living in that time when Satan has been loosed for a little while, as Revelation 20:3, 7-8 tells us.

CONCLUSION

So much more could be said about black magic and the occult. Whole bookstores are filled with its nonsense. The true answers are to be found in the Bible. Do we want power? Paul says, "For I am not ashamed of the gospel of Christ: for it is the power of God unto salvation to every one that believeth; to the Jew first, and also to the Greek," (Romans 1:16). Do we want knowledge? John says, "And hereby we do know that we know him, if we keep his commandments," (1 John 2:3). Let us teach our young people the Bible and give them the sword of the Spirit with which to combat the forces of evil.

WORKS CITED

Dictionary, The Magician's. http://www.crl.com/-tzimon/Magidict/magdic3.html

Freedland, Nat. The Occult Explosion. New York: Berkley Publishing Corp, 1972.

Gardner, Martin. Good, Bad, and Bogus. New York: Avon Books, 1981.

Greenwell, Richard J. Academia and the Occult: An Experience at Arizona. Vol. V. No. 1., Fall, 1980.

Larson, Bob. Satanism: The Seduction of America's Youth. Nashville: Nelson, 1989.

Mather, George A. & Larry A. Nichols. Dictionary of Cults, Sects, Religions and the Occult. Grand Rapids: Zondervan, 1993.

Randi, James. Investigation of Psychics. The Skeptical Inquirer, Vol. V. No. 4, Summer 1981.

Chapter 5

Witchcraft

Jackie M. Stearsman

INTRODUCTION

The subject of witchcraft is not an easy topic to define or write about. The term and activities associated with it must be understood in a given historical setting. Some use the term as a synonym for the Occult. Others would limit it to nature worship or folk magic. It embodies much that is subjective in nature. A popular term today is "Wicca." These advocates may not follow in every detail what another group using the same term may practice. This should not surprise us, neither do those wearing the name Christian practice a uniform doctrine, although they make some claims that are identified with what the Bible teaches. However, unlike the Bible, Witchcraft (modern "Wicca") has no objective standard by which it may be justified. Therefore, the reader of this presentation must understand that some may question what is herein stated because what is stated may not harmonize with what may be found in the multiplicity of subjective positions not cited by this chapter.

When a dictionary for the present usage is consulted, we read the following: "Witchcraft 1. Magic; sorcery. 2. Wicca. 3. A magical or irresistible influence, attraction, or charm" (American). In the Thesaurus we have this: "The use of the supernatural to affect or predict events: sorcery, black magic, conjuration, diabolism, enchantment, magic, necromancy, thaumaturgy, witchcraft" (American). The same source states the following about Wicca: "1. A pagan nature religion having its roots in pre-Christian western Europe and undergoing a 20th-century revival, especially in the United States and Great Britain. 2. A group or community of believers or followers of this religion" (American).

Others in this volume are assigned the topics of "Mediums," "Black Magic," "Voodoo," and "Psychics." I will purposefully avoid these areas except where necessary to make clear an idea or position essential for this chapter on Witchcraft.

In the space allotted, we will do the following: (1) Show Difficulties Defining Witchcraft and, (2) Present an Historical Overview and Critical Evaluation of Witchcraft.

DIFFICULTIES DEFINING WITCHCRAFT

Problems are encountered when using the English word "Witch." We are told:

> "The word 'witch' seems to denote etymologically 'one that knows.' It is historically both masculine and feminine; indeed the Anglo-Saxon form wicca, to which the English word is to be traced, is masculine alone. 'Wizard' is given as masculine for witch, but it has in reality no connection with it. . . In Wycliff's translation of (Acts 8:9) Simon Magus is called "a witch" ('wicche'). Since the 13th century the word "witch" has come more and more to denote a woman who has formed a compact with the Devil or with evil spirits, by whose aid she is able to cause all sorts of injury to living beings and to things. The term 'witchcraft' means in modern English the arts and practices of such women" (Davies).

Since the English terms "witchcraft" and "witch" were unknown in Bible times, some would remove them completely from our English Bibles (Davis). Where the King James Version uses the word "witch," it is replaced in later versions with “a sorceress” or the practice of “magical arts” (Deut 18:10; Ex. 22:18). The Witch of Endor often comes to mind in this connection, but a closer analysis of this event presents us with “a woman with a familiar spirit.” This refers to one who is supposed to have the ability to compel the departed spirit to return and to answer certain questions. A modern English term would be “Necromancy.”

Again, we are told:

> “The word "witchcraft" occurs thrice in the King James Version. in (1 Sam. 15:23), ‘the sin of witchcraft’ should be as in the Revised Version margin, ‘the sin of divination,’ the latter representing the Hebrew word . . . generally translated ‘divination’; . . .The phrase "used witchcraft" (of Manasseh, 2 Chron. 33:16) is properly rendered in the Revised Version (British and American) ‘practiced sorcery,’ the Hebrew verb . . . being that whence the participles in (Exod. 22:18 and Deut. 18:10), translated in the King James Version ‘witch,’ are derived. . . The word translated in the King James Version ‘witchcraft’ in (Gal. 5:20) (pharmakeia) is the ordinary Greek one for ‘sorcery,’ and is so rendered in the Revised Version (British and American), though it means literally the act of administering drugs and then of giving magical potions. It naturally comes then to stand for the magician's art, as in the present passage and also in Wisd. 12:4; 18:13; and in the Septuagint of (Isa. 47:9), where it represents the Hebrew noun . . . translated ‘sorceries’. . . The plural ‘witchcrafts’ (in the King James Version and the Revised Version (British and American) stands for the Hebrew noun just noticed in (2 Kings 9:22; Micah 5:12; Nah. 3:4), but in all three passages a proper rendering would

> be 'sorceries' or 'magical arts.' "Witchcrafts" is inaccurate and misleading" (Davies).

I continue to cite this source because it would be largely acceptable to those studying Bible concepts and ideas, especially from a conservative vantage point. In those passages where the plural "witchcrafts" appears in the King James Translation the ideas of "sorceries" or "magical arts" is the idea. Davies feels that "witchcraft" is inaccurate and misleading. After all the protesting of the use of the English term "Witch" and "Witchcraft," we are told:

> "Magic: Though the conceptions conveyed by the English word 'witch' and its cognates were unknown to the Hebrews of Bible times, yet the fundamental thought involved in such terms was familiar enough to the ancient Hebrews and to other nations of antiquity (Babylonians, Egyptians, etc.), namely, that there exists a class of persons called by us magicians, sorcerers, etc., who have superhuman power over living creatures including man, and also over Nature" (Davies).

Let us make some observations by way of comparison. Some "scholars" writing on the subject of worship tell us that since "worship" is not in the original language of the Bible, it is not proper to speak about the subject of worship except in a subjective manner. They further inform us that there are a number of terms that the English Bible renders "worship" that are not always translated worship. True, the Bible was not written in English. Therefore, we should not expect to have English terms in the Bible (Aramaic, Hebrew, Greek were the languages of the original) text. For our study, the question to be asked and answered is this: "Does the term 'witchcraft' contain a broad enough base to represent what is described in another language as 'Sorcery,' 'the worship of a plurality of gods,' 'the worship of Nature,' 'necromancy,' 'consulting mediums,' 'interpreting omens,' etc.?" Indeed it does, read again the quotes above about witchcraft.

If we are to use the word "witchcraft" today, it may be necessary to further qualify what we mean by the term. For example on the back cover of a modern publication, we read the following: "The practice of Wiccan magic is not evil, it is not supernatural. It is the creation of positive personal and global change through natural energies found in each of us and in the Earth. It is religion based on harmony with Nature Forces and all aspects of the Divinity" (Cunningham). Inside the front cover these two paragraphs appear:

> "For centuries, organized religions have perpetuated lies about the ancient practice of Witchcraft. To this day, many misinformed people think that 'Witches' worship Satan, perform human sacrifices, participate in sex orgies, and use drugs. In The Truth About Witchcraft Today, Scott Cunningham puts these common misconceptions to rest by showing that Witches are women and men from all walks of life, cultural backgrounds and religious upbringings. They have found Wicca (Witchcraft) to be the only religion that encourages love for the Earth and reveres the Feminine aspect of the Divine: the Goddess–an element missing in most other religions" (Cunningham).

While it is the case that some may have this form of "Witchcraft," it by no means follows that this is the exclusive use of the term. Are we to understand that today no one "claims" to delve into "deviate" behavior as practitioners of "black magic?" All that is needed to prove this is to read current publications and watch the news media as pockets of foolishness are exposed that do indeed practice rituals with a "claim" of producing more than "natural" effects upon others. In fact subjective writing abounds in the Cunningham volume. How are we to understand, in a consistent manner, the following: "Women, especially, are drawn to it [Wicca] because of its acceptance of the feminine aspect of Divinity–the Goddess. For Wiccans, theirs is the only religion that allows a truly intimate line with Deity." A few lines later: "Most Wiccans are intelligent enough to realize that their religion isn't the only path to Deity–a trait shared with few members of other religions" (Cunningham 5). Questions: (1) What are we to understand by the capitalized term "Deity" and "Divine"? If all is nature, there can be no Divine, no deities, except that which is manufactured by the uninformed mind. (2) How can there be "the only religion that allows a truly intimate link with Deity"? If all is nature, how can nature have a link with herself? (3) How can there be "the only religion that allows a truly intimate link with Deity" and at the same time affirm, "that their religion isn't the only path to Deity"?

Some may assert that Witchcraft/Wicca is a harmless system of the worship of nature, but from the perspective of the Bible, Witchcraft/Wicca is a false system of religion that deceives people and keeps God's true message from being followed.

HISTORICAL OVERVIEW AND CRITICAL EVALUATION OF WITCHCRAFT

1. *The Nations of Israel and Judah*

The worship of nature was and is forbidden in the Bible. In the Old Testament the Nation of Israel received her religious mandates from the one true God. In these directives the worship of the creation was forbidden:

> "I am the LORD thy God, which brought thee out of the land of Egypt, from the house of bondage. Thou shalt have none other gods before me. Thou shalt not make thee any

graven image, or any likeness of any thing that is in heaven above, or that is in the earth beneath, or that is in the waters beneath the earth: Thou shalt not bow down thyself unto them, nor serve them: for I the LORD thy God am a jealous God, visiting the iniquity of the fathers upon the children unto the third and fourth generation of them that hate me, And shewing mercy unto thousands of them that love me and keep my commandments" (Deut. 5:6-10).

We must understand that any worship of creation was forbidden the ancient Hebrew people who came out of Egyptian bondage and formed the original people under the Law of Moses. Any attempt to make nature worship a part of acceptable religious practices that may be viewed as an innocent form of primitive religion was not, and is not, acceptable to the one true God.

We must understand that any form of religion (witchcraft/wicca) that would deceive us into having a Father and Mother God/Goddess is also false. Not only is it false but it stands under the anathema of the one true God. It may be attractive to some in the modern women's movement, but attraction to individuals is not the basis of acceptable religion.

We must also understand that the Bible, and the God of the Bible, does not permit us to have a multiplicity of ways in religious matters. God's way is not to be confused with one way among many ways of reaching and serving the "Divine." There is nothing wrong with teaching and practicing true religion. There is nothing wrong with proselyting individuals from man-made foolishness to religion that did not originate in man but has been given to man directly by God.

As a nation of people, false religious practices were classified as a capital offence and were punished accordingly. In that day God provided proof that a religion was false, and demanded that His people remove it from their midst. In Israel the Civil State and the Religious State were one. Civil leaders were to support the religious leaders and the judges and kings were to administer the religious and civil codes as God directed them. Do we not read the following:

> "When thou art come into the land which the LORD thy God giveth thee, thou shalt not learn to do after the abominations of those nations. There shall not be found among you any one that maketh his son or his daughter to pass through the fire, or that useth divination, or an observer of times, or an enchanter, or a witch, Or a charmer, or a consulter with familiar spirits, or a wizard, or a necromancer. For all that do these things are an abomination unto the LORD: and because of these abominations the LORD thy God doth drive them out from before thee. Thou shalt be perfect with the LORD thy God. For these nations, which thou shalt possess, hearkened unto observers of times, and unto diviners: but as for thee, the LORD thy God hath not suffered thee so to do" (Deut. 18:9-14).

A careful reading of Deuteronomy 13 will show how extensive this discipline was to be administered. Individual relatives were not exempt, neither were collective groups in a city. The individual and city was to be removed from the nation for practicing false religions. In fact the captivity of the nations of Israel by the Assyrians (II Kings 17), and Judah by the Babylonians (II Kings 24-25; Dan. 9:1-19) is shown to be directly related to the practice of false religion by the people. In the words of Prophet of Jehovah God, Jeremiah, we have this indictment: "A wonderful and horrible thing is committed in the land; The prophets prophesy falsely, and the priests bear rule by their means; and my people love to have it so: and what will ye do in the end thereof?" (Jer.5:30-31). Many years before the Prophet Isaiah spoke the mind of Jehovah God in these words: "Woe unto them that call evil good, and good evil; that put darkness for light, and light for darkness; that put bitter for sweet, and sweet for bitter! Woe unto them that are wise in their own eyes, and prudent in their own sight!" (Isa. 5:20-21).

2. *The New Testament*

The New Testament is the final and complete revelation from God to man. The writers of the New Testament were directed by the Holy Spirit in receiving and composing the final and complete truth from God to man (John 14:26; 16:13; 1 Cor. 2:10-13; 2 Pet. 1:20-21). This final and complete revelation from God to man is designed to provide us with all things necessary for true religion (2 Tim. 3:16-17; Eph. 1:3; 2 Pet. 1:3). Today, the New Testament is the binding directive upon all people in all places and for all time (Matt. 28:18-20; Mark 16:15-16; Acts 17:30-31;Gal. 1:6-9). All religious matters are to be evaluated by this objective truth (1 Thess. 5:21-22; 1 John 4:1; 2 John 9-11; Gal. 1:6-9).

Since we are living under the New Testament, we are obligated to practice religion according to this model. Today, no individual is to practice paganism. Today, no individual is to practice the Old Testament Laws. The Old Testament Laws were true and binding upon Israel of old, but they are not binding on anyone today. This is an important distinction that some have not recognized in the past, and have made serious mistakes in religious matters.

God condemns the worship of creation today. God's wrath against the worship of creation and the failure to give glory to God is revealed in the Bible, and Paul writes of the downward spiral of paganism (Rom. 1:18-25; Acts 14:15-18).

In these same passages is condemned the idea of any other gods (male or female). It is false to assert that we are merely involved in innocent religious experimentation when we pervert the truth of the Bible and promote a "Divinity" that has a "Father God" and "Mother God." It is religious foolishness to talk about God or the Divine without having reference to the one true God of the Bible. Yes, we know that many make reference to God or the Divine with no objective basis. The Bible states that many will appear before Christ in judgment and make claims that they have done religious things in His name and will learn too late that He was never behind what they claim (Matt. 7:21-23). We may read of some self-styled exorcists who tried to use the name of Jesus to deceive the people into thinking they were practicing acceptable religion and found themselves exposed in the process (Acts 19:13-17).

3. *Church and State Relationship*

While the religious state and the civil state were united in the Old Testament directives to Israel, the church and state are separated today. God does not promote religion by the civil state. Religious instruction is to be done by the church and home. The state is to protect the good and punish the evil (Rom. 13:1-7; 1 Pet. 2:13-17). The New Testament knows nothing of a Christian Nation. The New Testament knows nothing of a leader in Rome that is both the civil leader and religious leader of all humanity. False positions have led to grievous errors in the past and could become equally damaging today if the truth is not known and practiced.

Jesus shows that He never intended for unbelieving people (whatever the source of their religious error nor the consequences of it) to be uprooted by physical force by the religious or civil communities. The words of the parable of the tares, and His interpretation need to be understood by all.

> "Another parable put he forth unto them, saying, The kingdom of heaven is likened unto a man which sowed good

seed in his field: But while men slept, his enemy came and sowed tares among the wheat, and went his way. But when the blade was sprung up, and brought forth fruit, then appeared the tares also. So the servants of the householder came and said unto him, Sir, didst not thou sow good seed in thy field? from whence then hath it tares? He said unto them, An enemy hath done this. The servants said unto him, Wilt thou then that we go and gather them up? But he said, Nay; lest while ye gather up the tares, ye root up also the wheat with them. Let both grow together until the harvest: and in the time of harvest I will say to the reapers, Gather ye together first the tares, and bind them in bundles to burn them: but gather the wheat into my barn. . . . [JESUS' APPLICATION] Then Jesus sent the multitude away, and went into the house: and his disciples came unto him, saying, Declare unto us the parable of the tares of the field. He answered and said unto them, He that soweth the good seed is the Son of man; The field is the world; the good seed are the children of the kingdom; but the tares are the children of the wicked one; The enemy that sowed them is the devil; the harvest is the end of the world; and the reapers are the angels. As therefore the tares are gathered and burned in the fire; so shall it be in the end of this world. The Son of man shall send forth his angels, and they shall gather out of his kingdom all things that offend, and them which do iniquity; And shall cast them into a furnace of fire: there shall be wailing and gnashing of teeth. Then shall the righteous shine forth as the sun in the kingdom of their Father. Who hath ears to hear, let him hear" (Matt. 13:24-30, 36-43).

These verses show us the will of God and Christ relative to false religions. As long as man has free will, he will depart from God and in doing so develop many false systems of religion. As damaging as false systems are, we are not authorized by God and Christ to remove false religion by force. The ultimate removal of false religions will be at the end of time and will be done so by Christ. However, this does not mean that we are to ignore false religion. We are to expose it and show the false premises upon which it is based. We must be like God, longsuffering and not willing that any should perish, but that all come to repentance based upon the true teaching of the Bible (2 Pet. 3:9). The New Testament abounds in examples where false religions were exposed. Peter withstood Simon who practiced sorcery (Acts 8). Paul exposed false religions in Athens (Acts 17). Paul confronted Peter when he failed to live up to the truth of the gospel (Gal. 2:11ff.). Paul warns about being deceived by false religious systems in Colossians 2, and Peter does the same in Second Peter 2. The words of Peter are much like the mandates in the Book of Jude.

God commands all men everywhere to repent (change the mind and reform the life). While it may be politically correct to practice religion as you choose, this does not mean that it is in harmony with the teachings of the Bible.

4. *Perverted Methods of Dealing With Witchcraft/Wicca*

The New Schaff-Herzogg Encyclopedia of Religious Knowledge, XII, pages 390-395, provides a detailed analysis of "Witchcraft and Witch Trials." However, for a brief and general summary more suitable for this chapter, we present the following:

> "The late medieval and early modern picture of diabolical witchcraft can be attributed to several causes. First, the church's experience with such dissident religious movements as the Albigenses and Cathari, who believed in

a radical dualism of good and evil, led to the belief that certain people had allied themselves with Satan. As a result of confrontations with such heresy, the Inquisition was established by a series of papal decrees between 1227 and 1235. Pope Innocent IV authorized the use of torture in 1252, and Pope Alexander IV gave the Inquisition authority over all cases of sorcery involving heresy, although most actual prosecution of witches was carried out by local courts.

At the same time, other developments created a climate in which alleged witches were stigmatized as representatives of evil. Since the middle of the 11th century, the theological and philosophical work of scholasticism had been refining the Christian concepts of Satan and evil. Theologians, influenced by Aristotelian rationalism, increasingly denied that "natural" miracles could take place and therefore alleged that anything supernatural and not of God must be due to commerce with Satan or his minions (see Aristotle). Later, the Reformation, the rise of science, and the emerging modern world—all challenges to traditional religion—created deep anxieties in the orthodox population. At the dawn of the Renaissance (15th century to 16th century) some of these developments began to coalesce into the "witch craze" that possessed Europe from about 1450 to 1700. During this period, thousands of people, mostly innocent women, were executed on the basis of 'proofs' or 'confessions' of diabolical witchcraft—that is, of sorcery practiced through allegiance to Satan—obtained by means of cruel tortures.

> A major impetus for the hysteria was the papal bull Summis Desiderantes issued by Pope Innocent VIII in 1484. It was included as a preface in the book Malleus Maleficarum (The Hammer of Witches), published by two Dominican inquisitors in 1486. This work, characterized by a distinct antifeminine tenor, vividly describes the satanic and sexual abominations of witches. The book was translated into many languages and went through many editions in both Catholic and Protestant countries, outselling all other books except the Bible" ("Witchcraft").

The potential for great harm abounds when religious superstition prevails. With little knowledge of the Bible text and no consistent principles of interpretation, foolishness is uncontrollable. The above historical facts will demonstrate this truth. Modern Wicca would not admit it, but the foolish subjective superstition advocated by them creates a world where all religions are on the same plane. With this world philosophy, no one religion may justify itself above that of another. Such an environment will not provide a basis for objective opposition of foolish superstition such as the "witch trials" of the past. Promoting paganism does not produce a peaceful society and neither does perverted religions that gave rise to the "witch trials" of the past.

5. *Modern Paganism and Superstition*

The less exposure people have to the true content of the Bible, and a proper interpretation of the same, the more circus like will become the religious climate. As the sources cited above show, old pagan beliefs are very popular in America and Great Brittan today. The entertainment community has picked up on this interest and there are a number of programs that promote religious superstition. By superstition, I mean the following:

> "1. An irrational belief that an object, an action, or a circumstance not logically related to a course of events influences its outcome. 2. A belief, practice, or rite irrationally maintained by ignorance of the laws of nature or by faith in magic or chance. A fearful or abject state of mind resulting from such ignorance or irrationality. Idolatry" (American).

Do the cable channels in your area carry "The Psychic Channel" today? Do those on the psychic channel try and convince you that psychic powers and psychic predictions have been confirmed? Are there programs that present "paranormal" events? What is fundamental to the following programs: "Buffy the Vampire Slayer," "Charmed," "Unsolved Mysteries," "Sightings," "Psychic Friends," "The X-Files," et al?

For critiques of the fascination with the "paranormal" you may wish to consult the skeptical Publishers, Prometheus Books. They have a volume Psychic Sleuths, edited by Joe Nickell. The Book jacket has this to say about the editor: "Joe Nickell, Ph.D., is a former stage magician and private investigator who has been featured in Discovery, Omni magazine and Scientific American. He now teaches technical writing at the University of Kentucky, where he is Writing Program adjunct to the College of Engineering." The jacket of the book states its purpose to be as follows:

> "Psychic Sleuths is an in-depth look at those who supposedly use extraordinary powers to help solve crimes. Investigative writer Joe Nickell has put together a special "task force" of experienced researchers–professional magicians, private detectives, paranormal investigators, and writers on pseudoscience–each of whom examined the

claims of a famous psychic crimebuster and reported on him or her at chapter length."

This source does not present a Biblical perspective on such foolishness. However, it is valuable for it shows the trickery and lack of proof of the claims of modern day superstition. I find it interesting that some of these skeptics are professional magicians. As the old adage goes, "takes one to know one."

CONCLUSION

In keeping with our assigned subject, we have refined the definition of witchcraft to the more contemporary aspects of witchcraft commonly called Wicca. However, we have shown that Wicca is not new. The leading feature of modern day American Witchcraft (Wicca) predates Christianity.

We have shown that both the Old Testament and the New Testament condemns the worship of nature and all efforts to worship a plurality of gods, whether male or female. In the religion that God gave Moses for the original people of Israel, it was a capital offense under their Law to practice false religions. The civil and religious courts were to act in such a way as to rid the people of false religions. It has also been shown that in the New Testament, the Law of God for all humanity today, false religion is not to be removed by force by either civil or religious groups. However, although false religion is permitted to exist without extermination, this in no way sanctions false religions. We bring this study to close with the following argument: All religions that teach that there are a plurality of gods (Deities, a mother god and father god), and that worship nature are false religions and are condemned by the Bible.

Wicca is a religion that teaches that there are a plurality of gods (Deities, a mother god and father god), and that worships nature.

Therefore, Wicca is a false religion and is condemned by the Bible.

WORKS CITED

American Heritage Talking Dictionary, CD-ROM. Learning Company, 1997.

Cunningham, Scott. The Truth About Witchcraft Today. St. Paul: Llewellyn, 1997.

Davies, T. Witton, "Witch, Witchcraft" International Standard Bible Encylopaedia, CD-ROM. Seattle, Biblesoft, 1996.

Jackson, Samuel Macauley, ed. New Schaff-Herzog Encyclopedia of Religious Knowledge. Grand Rapids: Baker, 1964.

Nickell, Joe, ed. Psychic Sleuths. Buffalo: Prometheus, 1994. "Witchcraft" Encarta 97 Encyclopedia, CD-ROM. Microsoft, 1996.

Chapter 6

Numerology

Howard Johnson

BIBLE CODE CRAZE

On November 4, 1995, the world was shocked to learn that Israeli Prime Minister Yitzhak Rabin had been assassinated. It was even more surprised to learn that a year earlier a reporter, Michael Drosnin, had told the Prime Minister of his impending doom. Drosnin claims it was revealed to him by a careful study of the Old Testament Scriptures using a 'Bible code.' Drosnin's claim, he says, involved a careful examination of the original text, and a calculated prediction, all ending in an apparent fulfillment (11-13).

What is this 'Bible code?' Can it really predict the future? Is there a way to assemble letters or numbers to predict the future? Can we really know what is on the morrow? These are questions the modern day seekers try to answer. Do all of these events truly equal a way to tell the future, or are they merely a profound coincidence? It has been suggested that Drosnin's 'Bible Code' discoveries could have saved the life of Rabin. If heeded, he would still be alive.

This is just one example of the growing hysteria over the possibility of new revelations coming from the Bible. However, what is being used today to extract information from the text of the Bible is not really new. The methods currently being employed are as old as man himself.

In the course of this study we will examine the historical background on this modern day phenomenon, its basic ideology, and finally, close with a tried and true pattern for finding "What saith the Lord."

DEFINITIONS

Some definitions are necessary before we can go further:

Cabala (Kabbalah): Jewish Mysticism. A practice of allocating number values to letters of the Hebrew alphabet and used to reinterpret the Old Testament — a forerunner to numerology (Tresidder 146).

Divination: to learn of the future, or of the unknown, by use of the occult. The word infers that the knowledge gained comes from the divine; from the gods (Buckland 29).

Gematria: the interpretation of a word according to the numerical value of its letters (Silver 413).

Numerology: use of numbers to interpret a person's character or divine the future. The theory behind numerology is based on the Pythagorean idea that all things can be expressed in numerical terms because they are ultimately reducible to numbers. Using a method analogous to that of the Greek and Hebrew alphabet (in which each letter also represented a number), modern numerology attaches a series of digits to an inquirer's name and date of birth and from these purports to divine the person's true nature and prospects (Britannica, 829).

Pythagoras: sixth century B.C. Italian philosopher. Developed the theory that numbers are things — that is to say that the nature of reality is number. This is not to be understood as to refer to Arabic or Roman numbers, but to gnomic or forms (Persons 629-30).

HISTORICAL BACKGROUND OF NUMEROLOGY

Numerology's origin is somewhat a mystery. Some have suggested it had its beginning in ancient Babylon, while others want to give it a relatively recent beginning. Regardless of its true origin it has been a major influence on kings, statesmen, and the great minds of history.

About 3000 B.C., the Sumerians established the sophisticated numbers system that has given us the sixty-minute hour and the sixty-second minute (Dodge 24).

Modern numerology contends that its history is based on 11,000 years of coincidence. It further contends to possess certain metaphysical capabilities to include: visualizing potential based on number analysis for the individual based on birth date, and name selection by the soul prior to birth to reflect the sound of its capabilities (Dodge 17).

The development and use of tarot cards as a way to divine the future were a direct outgrowth of numerology. It is believed that colored stones, then colored mosaics were tossed out at random and thus interpreted for the individual based on their position. It was later that numbers and images were added to the tiles.

Some would have us to understand that it was the Jewish people who kept the use of numerology pure, thus adding to the superstition that the code is preserved in the Old Testament text of the Bible. The cabala of the Jewish Talmudic scholars holds the key to interpretation of the Text (Dodge 25).

BASIC IDEOLOGY

As was noted in the introduction, there is an age-old philosophy that we can know the mind of God. As it relates to our subject of numerology, we can know truths of and about God that are not revealed by studying the words or contextual situations in the Bible.

As early as the Talmudic and Mishnaic period the feeling had prevailed in certain quarters that in addition to the literal meaning of the Bible (peshat) there was an allegorical meaning (derush). The cabalists went still further, and regarded the letters, words, and names of the Bible as possessed of deeply hidden divine mysteries, while such accounts as those of Hagar, Esau, and Balak contained far more than mere history. They therefore laid little stress on the literal sense of the Bible, though not a letter might be added to it or taken from it. In their endeavor to unlock the divine mysteries they employed various systems of exegesis. Of these the chief was germatria, or study of letters (Wunsche 328).

Even today some see the Bible as nothing more than a Ouija board, or a way to predict the future. It is concluded by these scholars that the Bible is full of continuous revelation, and it is only being revealed to those who are able to decipher the messages from beneath the words themselves—to go into the bible code.

Bob Larson, a noted expert on what is termed in today's culture as 'spiritual warfare' said in regards to the Bible's apparent predictive qualities:

Scripture attaches significance to certain numbers, but it fails to give numbers intrinsic predictive qualities. That notion comes from occult tradition and is based on impersonal principles of fatalism that contradict the Christian belief that grace is an aggressive act of God's love (253).

Furthermore, based on this 11,000 years of admitted coincidence the experts claim that "the divinations are always accurate, it is the interpretation by the reader which can be at fault" (Buckland 37). What a convenient approach—the educated guess principle. If your prediction did not come true then you misunderstood the signs.

This hysteria has grown to such a point today that normally rational thinking people are now looking for ways to determine their future. Many will now say yes, and say it confidently, when asked if the future can be had. With the apparent legitimizing of the discovery of a bible code the gates are open again for the accurate predicting of the future for mankind. Divination has been revived to aid us in discovering our Destiny.

Can man know what the future holds? Should Christians (children of God) be involved in the use of divination?

THUS SAITH THE LORD

It is obvious from this platform that some things must be assumed. Space does not allow for an exhaustive examination of the evidence. However, if we can agree that the Bible is a reliable, trustworthy, historical document, that it is a unity, and that it contains prophecy made and fulfilled, that it contains a view of man, the world, and an ethical standard above human invention, that it contains true accounts of miracles, that it presents the mission, authority, message, and commissioning of Jesus which are above human invention; THEN, the Bible is the inspired and authoritative revelation from God to man. Assuming all these are true let us continue.

But the Comforter, which is the Holy Ghost, whom the Father will send in my name, he shall teach you all things, and bring all things to your remembrance, whatsoever I have said unto you...Howbeit when he, the Spirit of truth, is come, he will guide you into all truth: for he shall not speak of himself; but whatsoever he shall hear, that shall he speak: and he will show you things to come (John 14:26, 16:13).

Jesus promised His disciples (future apostles) that the Comforter (Holy Spirit) would bring them (disciples — future apostles) into all truth, and that the Comforter would remind them of all things they had learned. In other words, the revelations concerning the kingdom of God would rest in the hands of the apostles.

Beloved, when I gave all diligence to write unto you of the common salvation, it was needful for me to write unto you, and exhort you that ye should earnestly contend for the faith which was once delivered unto the saints (Jude 3).

As Jude wrote the above words it was evident that his spirit was troubled. He had desired to send another message, a message that sounded their common bond — salvation, yet he felt compelled to write about the journey itself. Jude assured the saints that the saving message of the gospel of Jesus Christ had been delivered only once. A message not to be superceded. It was a message of hope that looked to a bright eternal day. It was a message revealed to God's saints. It was a complete message. The saints would have all they needed to prepare them for their journey. It was a message that they must strive after earnestly.

I marvel that ye are so soon removed from him that called you into the grace of Christ unto another gospel: {7} Which is not another; but there be some that trouble you, and would pervert the gospel of Christ. {8} But though we, or an angel from heaven, preach any other gospel unto you than that which we have preached unto you, let him be accursed. {9} As we said before, so say I now again, If any man preach any other gospel unto you than that ye have received, let him be accursed (Galatians 1:6-9).

Paul, a first century contemporary with Jude, informed the saints of Galatia that they should be aware of any teaching that contradicted his message.

The point to be made from these three passages is that if a message is different than what was once delivered to the saints of the first century it is to be rejected, because it does not come from God. It does not even allow for additional information.

Furthermore, this New Testament revelation was to supercede the Old Testament. Jesus Christ promised to fulfill that law and thus nailed it to the cross with his death (Colossians 2:14). The Old Testament law was a schoolmaster to bring man to the Christ, the Messiah, the Son of God (Galatians 3:24,25). That is not to say it is of no value to us today, just that its authoritative and predictive work ended at the cross. The Old Testament is still a profitable tool for us today. "For whatsoever things were written aforetime were written for our learning, that we through patience and comfort of the scriptures might have hope" (Rom 15:4 KJV). The Old Testament brings us comfort and hope in knowing assuredly that God is the same yesterday, today and forever.

God has always expected man to search for Him, and Him only to serve (Exodus 20, 1 Samuel 7:3, Matthew 4:10, Luke 4:8). God has always expected man to heed His warnings and instruction, with chaos and or destruction in the path of those who resist. God has always expected man to seek His wisdom, to seek His ways, to know that God would reveal all that man needed to be fully equipped unto every good work.

Man does not need to look to the stars, moon, or sun to find God's will for him. Man does not need to hope for or search the inner text of God's Revelation for hidden meanings or insight into the future. It is all in plain view. The Bible was written in a way that the common man could understand it. It was illustrated with real people, places, and things that we could relate to. God expects us to read, think, meditate on His word, and in it we may have that blessed hope of eternal life.

OLD TESTAMENT EXAMPLE OF DIVINATION

Saul with the witch of En-dor has led many to believe not only that it is possible to divine the future, but that God would allow such divination to be acceptable (1 Samuel 28). Samuel the prophet had died, and Saul was in need of wisdom in preparation for battle. God had also forsaken him and Saul did not know which way to turn. He approached a woman with a familiar spirit in hopes of contacting the wisdom of God in the matter. According to her divining, the witch supposedly conjured up the spirit of the dead prophet, Samuel. In this session the spirit of Samuel told Saul that the nation and he and his sons would fall victim to the Philistines. Some Bible scholars actually suggest that Samuel appeared to Saul at this event. However in light of such passages as: Leviticus 20:6, Deuteronomy 18:9-12, 1 Chronicles 10:13, I find it impossible to accept.

MODERN DAY DIVINERS

On at least two occasions in the book of Acts we see those who practiced the curious arts. In Acts 8:9ff we meet a sorcerer named Simon. It was said of him by the people of Samaria that he possessed the great power of God (v10). Yet it was at the preaching of the gospel that Simon learned the truth. He forsook his ways and was baptized into Christ (v13).

In Acts 18:19, an entire city burned the books of their curious arts. With the abundance of books of all types of subjects, especially those that promote the use of divination, maybe it is time we have a good old fashion book burning too.

The key ingredient in both of these Bible examples is that God expects us to be obedient in order to inherit His rewards for us (Acts 8:13; 18:20). It is not just a matter of accepting God as the Supreme Creator and then manipulating His message to suggest an ability to predict the future that is exclusive to the learned ones.

The world of the 20th century is not immune to the work of divination, especially in the name of religion. The great doomsdayers and modern day prophets continue to manipulate the Word of God to support their views of end time events. They claim a special revelation and understanding of the Scriptures to the exclusion of the majority. They have amassed entire armies of believers based on new revelations concerning numbers, weeks, horns, measurements, etc. in the Bible. By what I call 'doing the math' they profess the number to be a particular man, when in reality the number 666 reflects the inability of man to be like God — he comes short (Romans 3:23). Furthermore, they claim to be able to see the 'signs of the times', thus confidently knowing when the end will come.

God is no respecter of persons (Acts 10:34; James 3:17). He does not give special attention or impart special revelation to any select group today. God did not say that deep within the original texts you will find words or symbols that save you, but He did say "He that rejecteth me, and receiveth not my words, hath one that judgeth him: the word that I have spoken, the same shall judge him in the last day" (John 12:48). God's Word is for all and is subject to no private interpretation (2 Peter 1:20,21).

CONCLUSION

The subject of numerology has sparked renewed interest in an age old theory. However, it has done so by carrying simple ideas to their extreme. To say that numbers have no meaning in the Bible would be a false statement. To go further and say that numbers have a meaning beyond the written text would also be false. God has used numbers in the Bible to express power and wisdom. Those numbers when properly understood in their context will build faith in the one seeking God. Those numbers have no special power or carry any special meaning in themselves.

Numerology is a fascinating subject, one that can easily draw in the unsuspecting by its illusionary qualities. By using the Bible (God's

Word), once again Satan is able to draw men away (you shall not surely die — Genesis 3:4) from what is good, right, and true by preying on their sense that God is still revealing Himself today.

There will always be groups who will confess they know the mind of God better than others. Yet, after rational, balanced, and careful study we can know assuredly that words have meaning, the meaning God wants them to have, only in the context of His Holy Writ, the Bible.

In closing let me offer these final words from Jesus regarding the knowing of the future and how we should prepare ourselves for it.

Heaven and earth shall pass away, but my words shall not pass away. But of that day and hour knoweth no man, no, not the angels of heaven, but my Father only (Matthew 24:35,36).

THOUGHT QUESTIONS

1. If there was someone who could find new information using a bible code, what would they tell us about tomorrow? [consider James 4:13-15]

2. What comfort would God have provided the first century church, if the number 666 in Revelation 13:18 was a man in the 20th or 21st century?

3. If only 144,000 are going to heaven as some would have us to believe according to the book of Revelation, and if that is already accomplished [determined], then what hope do we have of ever seeing the Father, Son, or Holy Spirit face to face?

WORKS CITED

Buckland, Raymond. Here Is The Occult. New York: House of Collectibles, 1974.

Drosnin, Michael. The Bible Code. New York: Simon & Schuster, 1977.

Larson, Bob. Straight Answers on the New Age. Nashville: Nelson, 1989.

"Numerology." The New Encyclopedia Britannica. 15th ed. 1991.

Persons, Frederick T. "Pythagoreanism." Encyclopedia of Religion. Ed. Vergilius Ferm. New York: Philosophical Library, 1945. 629-30.

Silver, Abba H. "Kabbalah." Encyclopedia of Religion. Ed. Vergilius Ferm. New York: Philosophical Library, 1945. 412-13.

Tresidder, Jack. Dictionary of Symbols: an illustrated guide to traditional images, icons, and emblems. San Francisco: Chronicle Books, 1997.

Wunsche, August. "Cabala." The New Schaff-Herzog Encyclopedia of Religious Knowledge. Ed. Samuel MacAuley Jackson. Vol. 2. Grand Rapids: Baker Book House, 1963. 326-331.

Chapter 7

The Antichrist

Bobby Simmons

INTRODUCTION

There is a need to study and rightly understand who or what is an antichrist. This is true not only because it is a biblical subject, but also because of all the false and exaggerated teachings concerning the subject. The subject of the antichrist is no less important than any other biblical doctrine. We as students of the Bible need to properly understand the meaning that is to be conveyed by any and all scripture. The reason we study is because "profane and vain babblings" can bring about ungodliness and "overthrow the faith" of the believer.

> "Study to show thyself approved unto God, a workman that needeth not to be ashamed, rightly dividing the word of truth. But shun profane and vain babblings: for they will increase unto more ungodliness. And their word will eat as doth a canker: of whom is Hymenaeus and Philetus; Who concerning the truth have erred, saying that the resurrection is past already; and overthrow the faith of some" (2 Tim 2:15-18)

Second, we need to study this biblical subject so that we can answer in truth according to God's will those who lack knowledge and understanding, and thus we can help those who could be carried away with fables.

> "That I may make it manifest, as I ought to speak. Walk in wisdom toward them that are without, redeeming the time. Let your speech be alway with grace, seasoned with salt,

> that ye may know how ye ought to answer every man" (Col 4:4-6).

TRUTH AND OUR RELATIONSHIP WITH GOD

Truth directly affects one's relationship with God. Let's consider this relationship from a carnal point of view. Can one claim to be fully a part of a group or organization if that person opposes the teachings and beliefs of the organization that he/she desires to be a part of? The answer is obviously no. In order to be a part of anything, one must be willing to give themselves over to the abiding of the guidelines, rules, charters, etc., that govern the organization. The same is true of one who would be a part of the Lord's church. Jesus said of himself, "I am the way, the truth, and the life: no man cometh unto the Father, but by me. If ye had known me, ye should have known my Father also: and from henceforth ye know him, and have seen him" (John.14:6-7).

The way (or entrance) into His kingdom is established. The truth (governing authorities) of His kingdom is established, the life (consequence of actions) is established. The need for man's intervention regarding these truths is non-existent. The dependence between learning biblical truth and our relationship with God is so directly affected that we can ascertain the need to rightly learn and teach on this or any other subject.

In the course of this study we will be examining the truths taught concerning the antichrist. We will look at: *What is an antichrist? Is the antichrist easily recognized by his teaching and actions? Is the antichrist one or many?*

WHAT IS AN ANTICHRIST?

We live in a time in which there are a great number of religious bodies and teachings. Because of these differing beliefs there are a considerable number of descriptions and teachings pertaining to the antichrist. While these various teachings are interesting, it is not our intent to become a direct argument against all exaggerated and false teachings concerning the subject of the antichrist.

Some teachings regarding "antichrist" are so sensational that those who animate such teachings should be writing science fiction novels. The best way to dispel an erroneous teaching is not to address the false teaching, but rather teach what is true, allowing truth itself to expose error.

The term antichrist is used only four times in the New Testament, (1 John 2:18 & 22, 4:3; 2 John 7). It is translated from the Greek word "antichristos". There are several sources of good definitions we can consider:

- **Holman Bible Dictionary** — a particular individual or a group of people who oppose God and his purpose. Quite surprisingly, the word, "antichrist" appears only four times in the New Testament and there only in the Johannine epistles (1 John 2:18,22; 4:3; 2 John 7). It is a rather late term in Christianity, although its origin can be traced back to the Old Testament book of Daniel. In that Old Testament apocalypse, the term antichrist appears in two forms: 1) an individual who opposes God, or 2) a collective antichrist.
- **Thayer's Greek-English Lexicon of the New Testament** — of the corrupt power and influence hostile to Christian interest, especially that which is at work in false teachers who have come from the bosom of the church and are engaged in disseminating error.
- **Strong's Exhaustive Concordance** — an opponent of the Messiah.
- **Davis Dictionary of the Bible** — antichrist - against or

> instead of Christ...the word antichrist may mean as the etymology shows, an enemy of Christ or a usurper of Christ's name and rights.

It can be concluded that an antichrist is a person who opposes, directly or indirectly, by means of open opposition or by less obvious means, who may or may not have been a part of the Lord's church. His teachings vary from an outright contradiction of the gospel of Jesus Christ to a manner that is devised so as to deceive by means of twisting the truth.

While these definitions seem be to within the description and definition of Bible evidences, the Bible itself should always be the primary choice of reference to it's subject matter. Let's now begin to examine the Biblical description of the antichrist.

> "Little children, it is the last time: and as ye have heard that antichrist shall come, even now are there many antichrists; whereby we know that it is the last time. They went out from us, but they were not of us; for if they had been of us, they would no doubt have continued with us: but they went out, that they might be made manifest that they were not all of us. But ye have an unction from the Holy One, and ye know all things. I have not written unto you because ye know not the truth, but because ye know it, and that no lie is of the truth. Who is a liar but he that denieth that Jesus is the Christ? He is antichrist, that denieth the Father and the Son. Whosoever denieth the Son, the same hath not the Father: (but) he that acknowledgeth the Son hath the Father also. (1 John 2:18-23)

The antichrist at the time of the writing of the Bible was thought by many to be yet in the future, while John stressed they (being many) are with us now (vs 18). It even further noted that those who were to be known as antichrist had in fact once been part of them (part of the church).

John would further define this class as those who are liars, in that they would openly deny that Jesus was in fact the Christ, the messiah of Old Testament prophecy. While we may be able to give a simple definition to define what is a lie — the false and/or misrepresentation of truth — identifying a liar is a much more difficult task. The apostle Peter warned the Christians of such people in 2 Peter 2:1-3:

> "But there were false prophets also among the people, even as there shall be false teachers among you, who privily shall bring in damnable heresies, even denying the Lord that bought them, and bring upon themselves swift destruction. And many shall follow their pernicious ways; by reason of whom the way of truth shall be evil spoken of. And through covetousness shall they with feigned words make merchandise of you: whose judgment now of a long time lingereth not, and their damnation slumbereth not."

As we examine this text in light of our definition for an antichrist we indeed find many similarities. These false teachers were those who would deny the Lord who bought them and covet for themselves. The most damaging evidence that these too are antichrist is there regard for the truth, more particularly "the way of truth" and the fact that would speak evil of it. Jude also describes people with these same characteristics; "Beloved, when I gave all diligence to write unto you of the common salvation, it was needful for me to write unto you, and exhort you that ye should earnestly contend for the faith which was once delivered unto the saints. For there are certain men crept in unawares, who were before of old ordained to this condemnation, ungodly men, turning the grace of our God into lasciviousness, and denying the only Lord God, and our Lord Jesus Christ" (Jude 3,4). It can be seen that it is not necessary to refer to everyone as an antichrist who meets the profile of an antichrist. These false teachers who teach error meets the qualification to be categorized as a "liar" and an "antichrist”.

To identify someone who could be categorized as an antichrist because of his denial of Christ might seem to be a simple task. The truth is that a person can deny Jesus even if he or she acknowledges that God is.

> “Unto the pure all things are pure: but unto them that are defiled and unbelieving is nothing pure; but even their mind and conscience is defiled. They profess that they know God; but in works they deny him, being abominable, and disobedient, and unto every good work reprobate” (Titus 1:15-16)

Believing in God is more than a simple confession that He exists. From Titus, we can learn that a simple confession of God does not by itself constitute belief. "But in works they deny him" and "unto every good work a reprobate". James teaches this same truth but in a more detailed way, "What doth it profit, my brethren, though a man say he hath faith, and have not works? Can faith save him?" (James 2:14). James, being inspired of the Holy Ghost, instructs Christians that being able to say "I have faith" is not biblical faith at all. That in fact, there is an action which is required to accompany belief or faith. Action must accompany faith "thou believest that there is one God; thou doest well: the devils also believe, and tremble." (James 2:19). Based on the previous text to merely believe and called that biblical faith is as much a lie as to say Jesus is not the messiah. The work’s of man (those designed to elevate man) cannot be an expression of true faith. However to not have the good works that come from God announces to the world that you are not from God and thus spiritually dead (Titus 1:16, James 2:26).

From the Bible we've determined that any who would deny Christ, is in fact an antichrist. It has also been determined that denying Christ is more than not acknowledging him. An antichrist can be one who has confessed Christ but refuses to live a godly life as instructed by Him.

Remember what Peter taught regarding those that had been "bought" by Christ. Even after Jesus had paid the price on the cross of Calvary (2 Peter 2:1-3), these false teachers turned away from truth and begin to preach "feigned" words, even **denying Jesus**. They obviously knew Christ. The only logical explanation for them to be able to "deny" Christ is their turning from works that they had been ordained to do. All Christians are to be responsible to do the things our Lord has instructed us to do.

> "For the grace of God that bringeth salvation hath appeared to all men, Teaching us that, denying ungodliness and worldly lusts, we should live soberly, righteously, and godly, in this present world; Looking for that blessed hope, and the glorious appearing of the great God and our Saviour Jesus Christ; Who gave himself for us, that he might redeem us from all iniquity, and purify unto himself a peculiar people, zealous of good works" (Titus 2:11-14)
>
> "For we are his workmanship, created in Christ Jesus unto good works, which God hath before ordained that we should walk in them" (Eph.2:10)

JESUS IS THE CHRIST

John also wrote that an antichrist is one who denies either God the Father or God the Son (1 John 2:22). There are those who deny that God was manifested in the flesh. To do so is to deny both the Father and the Son. By biblical definition, this denial defines such a one as an antichrist. The Bible states that Jesus Christ is God the Son. Now while it may not be possible to fully explain all things pertaining to the trinity of the Godhead, we certainly are not left without explanation in regards to Jesus Christ as being a part of the Godhead. The gospel of John teaches this truth concerning Jesus and the Godhead.

> "In the beginning was the Word, and the Word was with God, and the Word was God. The same was in the beginning with God. All things were made by him; and without him was not any thing made that was made" (John 1:1-3 KJV).

The book of Colossians refers to the Son of God as being the Creator of all things.

> "Who hath delivered us from the power of darkness, and hath translated us into the kingdom of his dear Son: In whom we have redemption through his blood, even the forgiveness of sins: Who is the image of the invisible God, the firstborn of every creature: For by him were all things created, that are in heaven, and that are in earth, visible and invisible, whether they be thrones, or dominions, or principalities, or powers: all things were created by him, and for him: And he is before all things, and by him all things consist" (Col. 1:13-17)

Based on Peter's confession, Jesus admitted to his disciples that he was indeed the Christ, the Son of the Living God (Matt 16:16,17)

To deny the Deity of Christ or any portion of truth from him or about him is to be encompassed in the biblical definition of who is an antichrist. No statement can more lay to rest pertaining to Christ's Deity than that which Jesus made pertaining to himself, "I and my father are one" (John 10:17). To deny that Christ is as much deity as God the Father and God the Holy Spirit is to make one an antichrist.

ANTICHRIST - ONE OR MANY?

There are many teachings from various religious doctrines concerning an antichrist that is to rise up out of the sea of humanity just prior to Christ's Second Advent. He is to be embodied in the exact spirit of Satan. Some refer to him as the "son of Satan" making argument that he will posses the powers to work great miracles bringing about devastation upon earth and its inhabitants. The Bible supports no such teaching as this.

As it has already been determined by scripture, the antichrist number can be one or many (1 Jn. 2:18). John states that in "the last time" which is in reference to the New Testament period or Christian dispensation there is to come "that antichrist", and also states "even now there are many antichrist." It has been resolved through scripture that any who oppose Christ or the truth about and by Christ is in fact an antichrist. Who or what then is "that antichrist?" John in his writing to the church does not attribute any peculiarities, characteristics, or special powers to "that antichrist" more so than those who are identified as "antichrists". Both are grouped together as those that oppose Jesus. The Bible instructs us about others, spoke of singularly, who comply with the criteria that confirms this one is an antichrist.

THE MAN OF SIN

In the writing of the apostle Paul in the epistle to the church in Thessalonica, he warns them about an individual who beyond doubt, is an antichrist.

> "Let no man deceive you by any means: for that day shall not come, except there come a falling away first, and that

> man of sin be revealed, the son of perdition; Who opposeth and exalteth himself above all that is called God, or that is worshipped; so that he as God sitteth in the temple of God, showing himself that he is God" (2 Th 2:3-4)

The man of sin, also called the son of perdition, will set himself as one who opposes God, exalts himself above God, demands worship, tries to assume the position of God, and proclaims himself to be God. Some serious Bible scholars make an attempt to define this "man of sin" as an institution rather than a man, it is clear that this is a person. But is he any different than those that John makes reference to? It can be seen from the five points of evidence above that this person's intent is not unlike the antichrist that John alludes to. His position is to counter God.

Is this person someone who is to make his appearance at some future time? What does the scriptures say? 2 Thess. 2:4 states in the present tense that this person opposed God and attempted to declare himself God. This is certainly someone who is of current time as Paul wrote, and of great influence and authority. Many believe this person to be one of the Caesars of Rome such as Caesar Nero who had Paul beheaded or possibly Caesar Domition who reeked great havoc among the Jews and Christians alike. Regardless of who he was, he was an antichrist.

THE BEAST'S OF REVELATION

In order to understand who or what are the "beast" and "another beast" spoken of in Revelation 13, it is imperative that we understand the scene that is taking place in Revelation chapter 12. We see a contention between the "woman" and the "dragon". The dragon we know to be Satan (Rev.12:9 - "and the great dragon was cast out, that old serpent, called the devil"), and the "woman" is the faithful of God,

(Rev.21:9 - "and there came unto me one of the seven angels which had the seven vials full of the seven last plagues, and talked with me, saying, come hither, I will show thee the bride, the lamb's wife"). Then in Revelation 12:17, we see a picture of the dragon being very angry because of his failure to destroy the woman. "And the dragon was wroth with the woman, and went to make war with the remnant of her seed, which keep the commandments of God, and have the testimony of Jesus Christ". Then come the allies of the dragon in chapter 13.

The beast described in Revelation 13:1 is given certain distinctive features that give answer to who or what the beast is; "And I stood upon the sand of the sea, and saw a beast rise up out of the sea, having seven heads and ten horns, and upon his horns ten crowns, and upon his heads the name of blasphemy." Consider the description of the dragon (Satan) in Revelation 12:3 "and there appeared another wonder in heaven; and behold a great red dragon, having seven heads and ten horns, and seven crowns upon his heads."

Both the beast and the dragon have equal number of heads and horns and both had crowns. Also notice the work of the beast in 13:6 "and he opened his mouth in blasphemy against god, to blaspheme his name, and his tabernacle, and them that dwell in heaven."

Whether the beast is an individual or an institution, it is without fail that which directly opposes God making it either an antichrist or of the spirit that antichrists operates within.

The description of the "another beast" that is spoken of in Revelation 13:11-18 is not unlike that of the first beast,

> "And I beheld another beast coming up out of the earth; and he had two horns like a lamb, and he spake as a dragon. And he exerciseth all the power of the first beast before him, and causeth the earth and them which dwell therein to worship the first beast, whose deadly wound was healed.

> And he doeth great wonders, so that he maketh fire come down from heaven on the earth in the sight of men, And deceiveth them that dwell on the earth by the means of those miracles which he had power to do in the sight of the beast; saying to them that dwell on the earth, that they should make an image to the beast, which had the wound by a sword, and did live. And he had power to give life unto the image of the beast, that the image of the beast should both speak, and cause that as many as would not worship the image of the beast should be killed. And he causeth all, both small and great, rich and poor, free and bond, to receive a mark in their right hand, or in their foreheads: And that no man might buy or sell, save he that had the mark, or the name of the beast, or the number of his name. Here is wisdom. Let him that hath understanding count the number of the beast: for it is the number of a man; and his number is Six hundred threescore and six. (Rev 13:11-18)

Let us notice some of the affinity between the first and second beast; 1) the ability to work the same power or influence, 2) desired to bring about false worship. There is a point though that is unique about this second beast. Where the first beast may or may not be a person, the second most definitely is a man (vs.18).

Many reason that the first beast was a government body such as the Roman government that required the Caesar to be worshiped, and that the second beast was those who enforced that worship or delivered punishment for those who refused the Caesar worship. Others believe the first beast to be the Roman Catholic Church and the second those in the hierarchy that teach and enforce its false doctrine. Regardless of whom or what these beasts are/were, they are embodied in the spirit of an antichrist.

CONCLUSION

Whether it is the one antichrist or many antichrists spoken of by John, the "man of sin" spoken of by Paul, or the "beasts" of Revelation, we need to know who or what is of an antichrist spirit. The manner in which they oppose Christ is not always obvious. Their means to deceive are great. They are successful in robbing a great many of the hope offered by God. Jesus warns us of such as these.

> "And then if any man shall say to you, lo, here is christ; or, lo, he is there; believe him not: for false christs and false prophets shall rise, and shall show signs and wonders, to seduce, if it were possible, even the elect" (Mark 13:21-22).

WORKS CITED

Davis, John D. Davis Dictionary of The Bible. Nashville: Royal Publishers, 1973.

Holman Bible Dictionary. CD Rom, Quickverse Bible Reference Collection, Parson's Technology, 1994.

Strong, James. Strong's Exhaustive Concordance. 36th Edition. Nashville: Abingdon, 1977.

Thayer, Joseph Henry. Thayer's Greek-English Lexicon of The New Testament. 6th Printing. Grand Rapids: Baker Book House, 1987.

Chapter 8

Demon Possession

Wayne Jackson

As one begins a perusal of the New Testament, he encounters an unusual phenomenon known as "demon possession." The first Gospel writer recorded these words: "And the report of him [Jesus] went forth into all Syria: and they brought unto him all that were sick, holden with divers diseases and torments, possessed with demons, and epileptic, and palsied; and he healed them" (Matthew 4:24, ASV).

From this point on, there are numerous references to "demons" or "demon possession" in the New Testament. [NOTE: "Devils," as found in the KJV, is an incorrect rendition. The Greek word for devil is *diabolos*. Other terms, *diamon* (found once) and *dimonion* (63 times), are transliterated as "demon(s)" in the ASV. There is only one devil, but many demons.]

Critics of the Bible, of course, allege that this is an example of the sort of gross superstition that characterizes the ancient volume. The following quote represents a typical atheistic approach to this matter:

> "Mark 5:1-13 relates an incredible story wherein Jesus casts out the 'devils' from an unfortunate man. He then causes the devils to enter, instead, a herd of swine, and the swine, thus bedeviled, race over a cliff, fall into the sea and drown. Fundamentalists would have us believe that this is a true story. That tells us a lot about fundamentalists. Belief in demons and fairies and goblins and dragons ended, for most people, ages ago, and is remembered only in some Fairy

> Tales. Such primeval superstitions should be left behind, in our colorful past, where they belong (Hayes 129-130)."

Even religious modernists are prone to dismiss the biblical accounts of demon possession. William Barclay wrote:

> "We need not argue whether demons were realities or not. One thing certain is that in the time of Jesus people believed in them with terrified intensity. If a man believes he is ill, he will be ill. If a man believed that he was demon-possessed, then, illusion or no, he was definitely ill in mind and body" (Barclay 26).

The Scottish scholar went on to concede that Jesus may have believed in demons, but that

> "He did not come into this world to give men medical knowledge, and there is no reason to think that his medical knowledge would be any more advanced than that of the people of his day" (Ibid. 27).

To suggest that such a comment is a reflection upon the deity of Christ is an understatement. The New Testament does not represent Jesus merely as believing in demons, but depicts Him actually speaking to these beings, and being spoken to by them. He even commanded demons to do certain things. Either these evil spirits were a reality, or else the biblical record is entirely wrong. There is no other way to view the matter. This sort of a priori dismissal of the historical record is typical of unbelief. The skeptic, and even those religionists who have been influenced by the rationalistic mode of thought, repudiate anything that is not consistent with current human experience. But such an ideology simply is not an intelligent basis upon which to establish conclusions. There is validity in the credibility of historical testimony. The reality of demon activity, therefore, is not to be determined upon the basis of twentieth-century experiences;

rather, it is grounded in whether or not the New Testament documents are credible.

While I do not have the space to explore this matter in depth, I would like to make this observation. In 1846, Simon Greenleaf, Dane Professor of Law at Harvard University, produced a work titled The Testimony of the Evangelists Examined by the Rules of Evidence Administered in Courts of Justice. Greenleaf was the greatest authority in the history of legal procedure on what constitutes evidence. His massive three-volume set, A Treatise on the Law of Evidence (1842-53), is, to this very day, a standard on the topic of evidence. Greenleaf argued in The Testimony—with dramatic authority— that the accounts of Matthew, Mark, Luke, and John passed the strictest tests of authenticity, and thus may be regarded as dependable (1903, pp. 1-54). And without controversy is the fact that these writers described cases of demonic activity during the ministry of Jesus.

THE ORIGIN OF DEMONS

The etymology of the term "demon" is rather obscure, but some have suggested that it comes from a Greek root meaning "to know," hence probably means "a knowing one" (Vine, 1991, 203). Vincent noted that Plato derived the term from daemon, signifying "knowing" or "wise" (Vincent 92). Ancient Greek writers suggested that the genesis of the term is to be found in the fact that these entities were considered to be "intelligent beings" (McClintock and Strong 2:639). I will not concern myself with a detailed discussion of how demons were perceived in the ancient world, except to say that they were seen as evil spirits "somewhere between the human and the divine" (Arndt and Gingrich 168).

Unlike the speculative literature of antiquity, the New Testament makes no attempt to explain the origin of demons or to describe any materialized features (cf. Reese 2:141). This appears to be significant; the restraint, I believe, is a subtle evidence of the divine inspiration of the narratives (see Jackson, 1996). Scholars, however, have speculated as to the origin of demons. I will briefly consider some of the ideas.

(1) Some claim that demons were the disembodied spirits of a pre-Adamic race of men who lived upon the Earth in a "gap period" that allegedly fits between Genesis 1:1 and 1:2. There are two things wrong with that notion: (a) There is absolutely no evidence that there ever was a historical "gap" between the first two verses of Genesis (see Fields, 1976). (b) There were no people before Adam. He came directly from God (Luke 3:38), and was the "first" man (1 Corinthians 15:45).

(2) Others trace the origin of demons to a supposed cohabitation between angels and certain women of the pre-Flood world (Genesis 6:1-6). This theory is negated by the fact that Christ taught that angels are sexless beings, incapable of such unions (Matthew 22:30; see also Kaiser 33-38).

(3) It has been argued that first-century demons may be identified with the fallen angels mentioned in 2 Peter 2:4 and Jude 6, some of whom, consistent with the divine plan, were permitted to leave temporarily that sphere of confinement for the purpose of inhabiting certain people. Charles Hodge argued this theory (Hodge 643), which probably is the most popular idea regarding this matter.

(4) Another view is that demons were the spirits of wicked dead men who were allowed by God to leave the Hadean realm to accommodate the implementation of the divine plan of redemption. Josephus claimed that demons were the "spirits of the wicked, that enter into men that are alive and kill them, unless they can obtain some help against them" (Wars 7.6.3). Alexander Campbell delivered a very

learned lecture in Nashville, Tennessee on March 10, 1841, in which he, in rather persuasive fashion, argued the case that the "demons" of the ancient world were the spirits of the dead. The printed form of that presentation is well worth studying (Campbell 379-402).

In the final analysis, no dogmatic conclusion can be drawn with reference to the origin of demons. That they existed admits of no doubt to anyone who takes the Bible seriously; as to their origin, the Scriptures are silent.

THE NATURE AND CHARACTER OF DEMONS

The nature of demons is spelled out explicitly in the New Testament. They were "spirit" beings. This, of course, creates a problem for the skeptic, who denies that there is anything beyond the material. But consider the testimony of Matthew. "And when evening was come, they brought unto him [Christ] many possessed with demons: and he cast out the spirits with a word..." (8:16). Note that the terms "demons" and "spirits" are used interchangeably. Since it is known also that "a spirit does not have flesh and bones" (Luke 24:39), one must conclude that demons were not physical beings.

As spirit entities, demons could exercise both volition ("I will return...") and locomotion ("Then goeth he...") (Matthew 12:44-45). Moreover, they could assimilate factual information. A demon once spoke to Christ and said: "I know thee who thou art, the Holy One of God" (Luke 4:34; cf. Mark 1:24). Too, they possessed a religious sensitivity. "Thou believest that God is one; thou doest well, the demons also believe and shudder" (James 2:19). "Shudder" suggests to "be struck with extreme fear, to be horrified" (Thayer 658). The fact is, they tremble in prospect of their ultimate doom (see Matthew 8:29).

As to their character, demons are depicted as "unclean" and "evil."

In describing the vile nature of the Jewish nation of His day, the Lord gave an illustration regarding a man who was possessed of an "unclean" spirit (Matthew 12:43); the spirit left the man, but eventually re-entered the gentleman, taking with him other spirits "more evil" than himself (vs. 45). This passage reveals the "unclean" (Greek *akathartos*—"not pure") or "evil" (*kakos*—that which not only is morally malignant, but injurious as well; cf. Vine, 1991, 272) disposition of demons. From this text it is observed also that there were degrees of vileness ("more evil") in demons.

THE EFFECTS OF DEMON POSSESSION

The physical and/or mental effects occurring in certain individuals as a consequence of being possessed by a demon or demons (more than one could in-dwell a person; Mary Magdalene had once been inhabited by seven demons—Luke 8:2) were varied. Some demoniacs were afflicted with blindness and/or the inability to speak (Matthew 9:32; 12:22).

Some thus possessed might be prone to violent convulsions. A case recorded by all three synoptic writers tells of a young man who was "epileptic." He suffered grievously, frequently falling into the fire or into water (Matthew 17:15). He was dashed to the ground and bruised badly (Mark 9:18; Luke 9:39); he foamed at the mouth, ground his teeth, and "pineth away" (Mark 9:18). This final descriptive may suggest that the boy's body became rigid so that he was incapable of motion (Arndt and Gingrich 550). A demon-possessed man who lived among the tombs on the eastern side of the Sea of Galilee had excessive strength. He often had been bound with chains and fetters, but he had broken these restraints into pieces, and no one had the power to tame him (cf. also Acts 19:16). Further, he was characterized by both emotional illness and antisocial behavior (e.g., he wore no clothes—Luke 8:27), but when Christ purged the demon from the poor fellow he was observed "clothed, and in his right mind" (Mark 5:15).

It is important to distinguish between cause and effect in these cases. The cause was that of demon possession; the effects were physical and/or emotional maladies. The Scriptures never confuse the two. In other words, "demon possession" was not just an ancient, unenlightened attempt to explain physical and/or mental problems. Rather, a clear distinction is made between being inhabited by an unclean spirit and being sick. Demon possession could produce illness, but not all illness was attributed to the indwelling of evil spirits. Note the distinction that is drawn in the following passage. "And at even, when the sun did set, they brought unto him [Jesus] all that were sick, and them that were possessed with demons" (Mark 1:32). The double use of the definite article (tous), together with the conjunction, reveals that two distinct classes are under consideration—those who were merely sick, and those who were demon possessed and may or may not have had attending problems. Lenski has commented:

> "Two classes are markedly distinguished; those suffering from ordinary diseases and those possessed with demons. The distinction shows that the latter cannot be classed with the former in spite of modern attempts in that direction" (Lenski 84).

THE DIVINE PURPOSE IN ALLOWING DEMON POSSESSION

The New Testament clearly indicates that demons were under the control of divine authority. Jesus, for example, could command them to leave a person (Matthew 8:16), or even to keep quiet (Mark 1:34). The demons that tormented the man in the country of the Gerasenes could not enter the nearby swine herd except by the Lord's concession

(Mark 5:13-14). Since it is the case that demons could do nothing except by divine permission, the intriguing question is: Why did God allow these malevolent beings to enter into people? The truth of the matter is, the Bible does not give a specific answer to this question—as much as our curiosity wants to be fed. I believe, though, that a reasonable case can be built to help shed some light on the subject. If the mission of Jesus Christ, as the divine Son of God, was to be effective, the Lord's absolute authority had to be established. No stone could be left unturned. Accordingly, we see the Savior demonstrating His authority in a variety of ways. (1) Christ exhibited power over diseases and physical ailments (Matthew 9:20-22; John 4:46-54; 9:1-41). (2) The Lord exerted His authority over material objects (Matthew 14:15-21; 17:24-27; John 2:1-11; 21:1-14). (3) Jesus showed that He could control the elements of nature (Matthew 8:23-27). (4) The Master even suspended the force of gravity with reference to His own body when He walked upon the waters of the Sea of Galilee (Matthew 14:22-23). (5) The Lord released certain ones who had been captured by death (Matthew 9:18-26; John 11:1-45). (6) Finally, it is not unreasonable to assume that, just as the Savior had displayed His marvelous power in all these realms, it likewise was appropriate that He be able to demonstrate His authority in the spirit sphere as well. Satan is not in full control! In fact, note this interesting passage. When the seventy disciples returned from an evangelistic trip (Luke 10:1), they joyfully proclaimed to Christ: "...Lord, even the demons are subject to us in thy name." Jesus responded: "...I beheld Satan fallen as lightning from heaven" (Luke 10:17-18). The significance of that statement is this: the disciples' power over demons, under the aegis of Christ's name (authority), was but a preview of the ultimate and complete fall of the devil. One scholar has expressed the matter in the following way.

> ...Jesus viewed the triumph of these [disciples] as being symptomatic of ever so many other victories over Satan throughout the course of the new dispensation, triumphs accomplished through the work of thousands of other missionaries. He was looking far into the future (cf. Matt. 24:14). He saw the ultimate discomfiture of the ugly dragon and all his minions (Hendriksen 581).

Consider another reference. Christ said: "But if I by the Spirit of God cast out demons, then is the kingdom of God come upon you. Or how can one enter into the house of the strong man, and spoil his goods, except he first bind the strong man?, and then he will spoil his house" (Matthew 12:28-29; Luke 11:20-22). The Savior's argument is: I have cast out demons, the servants of Satan. I could not have done so if I were not stronger than he is. My power thus is superior to his.

These passages, I believe, help us to understand the purpose of demon possession in the first century. It established the comprehensive and supreme authority of the Son of God. Why demons entered particular individuals is not explained in the Scriptures. Unger speculated that "in the great majority of cases possession is doubtless traced to yielding voluntarily to temptation and to sin..." (Unger 95). However, in the instance of the epileptic boy, the lad had been tormented "from childhood" (Mark 9:21), which suggests, at the very least, that personal sin was not necessarily a causative factor in demon possession.

CASES IN THE GOSPEL RECORDS OF JESUS' EXPELLING DEMONS

The demoniac in the synagogue (Mark 1:23; Luke 4:33-36). The Gerasene demoniac (Matthew 8:8:28-34; Mark 5:1-20; Luke 8:26-39). The Syrophoenician girl (Matthew 15:21-28; Mark 7:24-30). The epileptic boy (Mt. 17:14-21; Mark 9:14-29; Luke 9:37-43). The mute demoniac (Matthew 9: 32-34). The blind and mute demoniac (Matthew 12:22ff.; Luke 11:15).

A CONTRAST WITH PAGANISM

It is worthwhile to make this brief observation. The ancient world abounded with superstition relative to demons (where the genuine exists, the counterfeit will be as well). But there is a vast chasm between the accounts of demons in the New Testament and that of the pagan world and, in fact, even among some of the Hebrew nation. For instance, as mentioned earlier, there are no accounts in the New Testament of any visual descriptions of demons. Such characterizations, however, were common in the heathen world. A bronze statue from ancient Babylon contains the image of the demon Pazuzu. The figure has the wings and feet of an eagle, a human body with claws for hands, and a misshapen head (Aune 1:920).

Josephus tells of a demon expulsion whereby the exorcist,

> "...put a ring which had a root of one of those sorts mentioned by Solomon, to the nostrils of the demoniac, after which he drew out the demon through his nostrils..." (Antiquities 8.2.5).

The New Testament contains no such absurd concoctions.

DEMON POSSESSION TODAY?

Do evil spirits enter into human bodies and afflict people today? I confidently affirm they do not. Unfortunately, though, some modern writers have argued that demon activity is still a part of Earth's environment. Charles Ryrie contended that certain "fallen angels" are "still free to roam the earth as demons carrying out Satan's designs" (Ryrie 296). Merrill Unger, a respected scholar, subtitled his book,

Biblical Demonology, "A Study of the Spiritual Forces Behind the Present World Unrest." Several years ago a book titled UFOs, Satan and Evolution enjoyed a limited circulation in the evangelical community. Therein the author claimed that hundreds of UFO visits to Earth represented an invasion of demons. He cited one "example" where a demon raped a woman (an interesting feat for a spirit!). The fact that a prominent creationist wrote the Foreword for this literary fiasco remains an inexplicable mystery.

The position that demon possession does not exist today can be argued from a twofold base. First, a thoughtful study of the details associated with the so-called modern examples of demon habitation reveals that these cases bear no resemblance to the genuine examples of spirit possession described in the New Testament. The contrast is dramatic. Second, a consideration of certain data set forth in the New Testament leads only to the conclusion that demon possession was a first-century experience; it was allowed for a very specific reason, and the divine concession was suspended near the end of the apostolic era.

THE MODERN EXORCISM MANIA

When the movie, The Exorcist (based upon William Blatty's novel of the same name), made its appearance in December 1973, a wave of mystical excitement that has been dubbed "the exorcism frenzy," swept the nation. (By the time the movie had been out for 5 weeks, Blatty's book had sold 9 million copies.) Scores of people began to surmise that they were possessed of evil spirits—or that they knew someone else who was! Numerous articles regarding these alleged experiences appeared in mainline newspapers and magazines. A careful consideration of the details involved in these alleged episodes highlights some startling contrasts to the New Testament (cf. Woodward). Reflect upon the following differences.

(1) The "exorcisms" of today are performed almost invariably in dark, secluded environments, only to be publicized later. When Jesus cast out demons, the episodes were public, and therefore subject to critical examination (cf. Luke 4:31-37).

(2) The Lord could expel evil spirits with but a word, and the effect was immediate (Luke 4:36; Matthew 17:18). The Jesuit Priest who supposedly "exorcised" a demon from the youngster who served as the subject of Blatty's book, The Exorcist, confessed that it took him two months of preparation (fasting on bread and water), and twenty ritual ceremonies to purge the child.

(3) The demoniacs of the New Testament era were afflicted, either physically or mentally, by a malfunction of what were otherwise normal human traits. Those cases involved no grotesque details. However, according to Roman Catholic priest Luigi Novagese (the official exorcist for the papal diocese in Rome), "A man's skin turned white like paper, his teeth became transparent, his eyes bulged with balls of flame and fire issued from his mouth." One priest claimed that a demon took a bite out of his sandwich. The February 11, 1974 issue of Newsweek magazine carried a photo of the burglarized delicacy, displaying perfect, human-like teeth prints! Do demons get cavities?

(4) Modern demoniacs frequently are described as uttering "fierce curses" and "bursts of blasphemy." In the New Testament record, demons always were very respectful of deity (Mark 1:24; 3:11). There is not a solitary case of a demon blaspheming either God or Christ in the biblical narratives.

(5) Two cases of demon possession in the New Testament reveal that the unclean spirits could empower their hosts with supernatural strength (Mark 5:1-20; cf. Acts 19:13-16). The demoniac described in Mark 5 could not be bound even with a "chain." A respected university professor posed this interesting query:

> "If we have demon-possessed people today, why in my travels in over forty countries of the world have I never seen a person who is so strong that you can't bind him with chains (cf. Mk. 5:3)?" (Edwards 135).

(6) The ability to cast out demons in the first century was given in order to confirm the truth of the Gospel message (Mark 16:17-20). Modern "exorcists" preach everything but the Gospel.

A REASONABLE ARGUMENT

A powerful case can be made for the proposition that demon possession was not allowed to continue beyond the apostolic age—the era of miracles.

I first must mention that when the prophet Zechariah foretold the coming of the Messianic dispensation, and the blessings that would accompany the spread of the Gospel, he suggested that the Lord would "cause the prophets and the unclean spirit to pass out of the land" (13:1-2). Some feel that the expression "unclean spirit" may hint of, or at least include, the cessation of demonic activity. Hailey sees this as a prediction of the eventual termination of prophetic activity (on the part of God's people) and the curtailing of the power of unclean spirits. Likewise, unclean spirits, the antithesis of the prophets, would cease. In the conquest of Christ over Satan and his forces, unclean spirits have ceased to control men as they did in the time of the ministry of Christ and the apostles. . .(Hailey 392).

While this is not a common view of Zechariah's prophecy, and certainly not one upon which an entire case could be built, it is not without possibility. A firmer proposition can be argued as follows.

With the close of the first century, the age of the supernatural came to a close. God is not empowering men to operate in a miraculous fashion today. This is evinced in the following way:

(1) Nothing duplicating the miracles of the first century is apparent today. No one can walk upon water, raise the dead, calm a raging storm, turn water into wine, instantly heal an amputated ear, extract tax money from a fish's mouth, etc. Miracles are self-authenticating phenomena that cannot be denied, even by hostile critics (cf. John 11:47; Acts 4:14-16); clearly, they are not occurring today.

(2) The purpose of supernatural gifts was to confirm the authenticity of divine revelation being received from heaven (Mark 16:9-20; Hebrews 2:1-4). Since the revelatory process was completed when the last New Testament book was written, miracles no longer are needed, hence, have ceased. They were like the scaffolding that is removed once the building is finished.

(3) The New Testament explicitly argues that the day was on the horizon when miracles would cease. Paul defended that position both in Ephesians 4:8-16 and in 1 Corinthians 13:8-10. During the early days of the apostolic era, divine revelation had been "in part," i.e., piece-by-piece. The apostle said, however, that when "the perfect" or "the complete" arrived, the partial revelation, which came by means of the various "gifts" (e.g., supernatural knowledge and prophecy), would cease (1 Corinthians 13:8ff.). Prominent Greek scholar, W.E. Vine, summarized the matter well. With the completion of Apostolic testimony and the completion of the Scriptures of truth ("the faith once for all delivered to the saints", Jude, 3, R.V.), "that which is perfect" had come, and the temporary gifts were done away. For the Scriptures provided by the Spirit of God were "perfect". Nothing was to be added to them, nothing taken from them. This interpretation is in keeping with the context (Vine, 1951, 184). Elsewhere this writer has discussed the theme of miracles and their duration in much greater detail (Jackson, 1990, 114-124).

Here is a crucial point. If it is the case that miraculous powers have been removed from the church's possession, including the ability to cast out demons (Mark 16:17-20), does it stand to reason that God would allow demons to supernaturally assault people today, thus granting Satan an undue advantage over the human family? How would this square with the promise that, "... greater is he that is in you than he that is in the world" (1 John 4:4)? In other words, if the gift of expelling demons no longer is extant, is it not a reasonable conclusion that demon possession is obsolete as well?

CONCLUSION

Certainly Satan exerts great influence today. However, as God does not work miraculously in this age, but influences through his Word and through the events of providence, so also, the devil wields his power indirectly, and non-miraculously, through various media. Current cases that are being associated with demon possession doubtless are the results of psychosomatic problems, hysteria, self-induced hypnosis, deception, delusion, and the like. They have natural, though perhaps not always well understood, causes.

WORKS CITED

Arndt, William F. and F. Wilbur Gingrich. A Greek-English Lexicon of the New Testament. Chicago, IL: University of Chicago, 1967.

Aune, D.E. "Demonology," The International Standard Bible Encyclopedia—Revised, ed. Geoffrey Bromiley. Grand Rapids, MI: Eerdmans, 1979.

Barclay, William. And He Had Compassion—The Healing Miracles of Jesus Valley Forge, PA: Judson Press, 1976.

Campbell, Alexander. Popular Lectures and Addresses Nashville: Harbinger Book Club, n.d.

Edwards, Earl. "Powers of Darkness—Demon Possession," Settled in Heaven, ed. David Lipe Henderson, TN: Freed-Hardeman University, 1996.

Fields, Weston W. Unformed and Unfilled Nutley, NJ: Presbyterian & Reformed, 1976.

Greenleaf, Simon. The Testimony of the Evangelists Examined by the Rules of Evidence Administered in Courts of Justice Newark, NJ: Soney & Sage, 1903 edition.

Hailey, Homer. A Commentary on the Minor Prophets Grand Rapids, MI: Baker, 1972.

Hayes, Judith. In God We Trust: But Which One? Madison, WI: Freedom from Religion Foundation, 1996.

Hendriksen, William. An Exposition of the Gospel of Luke Grand Rapids, MI: Baker, 1978.

Hodge, Charles. Systematic Theology London: James Clarke, 1960 edition.

Jackson, Wayne. "Miracles," Giving a Reason for Our Hope, ed. Winford Claiborne, Henderson, TN: Freed-Hardeman College, 1990.

Jackson, Wayne. "The Silence of the Scriptures: An Argument for Inspiration," Reason & Revelation, 16:17-22, 1996.

Kaiser, Walter C., Jr. More Hard Sayings of the Old Testament Downers Grove, IL: InterVarsity Press, 1992.

Lenski, R.C.H. The Interpretation of Mark's Gospel Minneapolis, MN: Augsburg, 1964.

McClintock, John and James Strong, editors Cyclopedia of Biblical, Theological, and Ecclesiastical Literature Grand Rapids, MI: Baker, 1968 reprint.

Reese, David G. "Demons," The Anchor Bible Dictionary, ed. David Noel Freedman, New York: Doubleday, 1992.

Ryrie, Charles C. Biblical Theology of the New Testament Chicago, IL: Moody, 1959.

Thayer, J.H. A Greek-English Lexicon of the New Testament. Edinburgh: T.&T. Clark, 1958.

Unger, Merrill F. Biblical Demonology. Wheaton, IL: Scripture Press, 1952.

Vincent, Marvin Word Studies in the New Testament Wilmington, DE: Associated Publishers & Authors, 1972 edition.

Vine, W.E. First Corinthians—Local Church Problems. Grand Rapids, MI: Zondervan, 1951.

Vine, W.E. Amplified Expository Dictionary of New Testament Words. Iowa Falls, IA: World Bible Publishers, 1991.

Woodward, Kenneth L. "The Exorcism Frenzy," Newsweek, 83:60-66, 1974.

Chapter 9

Voodoo & Santeria

Brian Kenyon

Probably almost every adult in the Western world has at least heard of voodoo, although most of what they have heard undoubtedly has been "Hollywood's version." Fewer people have heard of Santeria. The study of voodoo and Santeria is needed because both religions exert a tremendous amount of influence in their native lands and abroad, especially in the United States, where freedom of religion has been a cornerstone philosophy.

In Haiti, people are taught from childhood to "honor their divinities. Parents use voodoo to teach their children how to behave and what the community expects of them" (Beckwith and Fisher 113). Voodoo's influence in the United States is well documented. For example, the March 6, 1999 issue of the Lakeland, Florida newspaper reported that a funeral home owner was convicted of "performing voodoo-like rituals on a dead man by putting pin-stuck dolls stuffed with cotton in his chest cavity and chopping off his hand" (Brooks).

In Cuba, Santeria's influence is seen almost everywhere. According to some estimates, the Cuban-based religion claims more than a hundred million practitioners in Latin America and the United States. One website consulted by this author boasted of one hundred thousand hits per month.

This study will not consist of an exactly parallel study of voodoo and Santeria. Rather, it will consist of an individual background study of both religions and an examination and evaluation of some of the more characteristic doctrines of voodoo and Santeria as viewed by this author.

BACKGROUND AND INFLUENCE OF PRE-LITERARY SOCIETY RELIGION ON VOODOO AND SANTERIA

To some, voodoo and Santeria may be thought of as "primitive" religion. However, contrary to popular thought, the oldest religion of humanity was monotheistic. Truly "primitive" religion is the belief in one, eternal God who created all things that were created, and to whom all people are accountable. The early chapters of Genesis show this to be true. Early in the history of humanity, the true God required his subjects to offer animal sacrifices on altars made of earth and unsculptured stones (Ex. 20:24-25 cf. Gen. 8:20; 12:7; 13:18; 26:25; 35:1). Because of this, absolutely no physical trace of "primitive" religion has survived for the archeologist to uncover. In time, however, monotheism of the true God evolved into monotheism of a false god which eventually evolved into polytheism. Since these departures involved complex rituals with elaborate paraphernalia, the archeologist can uncover physical evidence, and the anthropologist can claim that "primitive" religion was superstitious non-sense.

Because both voodoo and Santeria have their roots in African religion prior to the colonization of the Americas, it is necessary to give a background of "pre-literary society" religion. While this "pre-literary" religion is not confined to Africa, it is certainly found in Africa, even in the twentieth century. A "pre-literary society" may be defined as "a group of people who feel they belong together through sharing a common culture and set of values, a common territory and social organization, and probably a common language" (Newing 13). Although a majority of these pre-literary societies have ceased or have been radically altered by foreign influence over the last couple of centuries, some still continue in much the same way as they have for hundreds of years. To fully understand each pre-literary society, one must consider its language, social structure, religious personages, oral literature, prayers, music, rituals, artwork, sanctuaries, and taboos (things which are prohibited). Although one cannot stereotype all pre-literary societies, there are some common underlying principles of their religions that affect their views of reality. The following is a summary of these principles (adapted from Newing 31-37).

First, they have a holistic view of life. Everything is interconnected so that every activity from birth to death and the afterlife is interpreted as belonging to a religious whole. Second, phenomena are viewed as the workings of spiritual forces which permeate the environment. For this reason, fear (especially of the night) plays an important role. Death is usually ascribed to witchcraft. Third, myths (traditional stories) keep alive the legends of deity that each community values. All the great moments of life and death are given meaningful expression through these myths so that each person lives and shares in the life of the divine. Fourth, rituals based on myths reinforce the traditional ideals. These rituals are dependent upon the spiritual forces which govern the seasons. Fifth, time is not measured as linear but as cyclic. Time involves a series of cycles that occur over and over again. The importance of time is found in the seasons to which the sun, moon, and stars serve as reference. Rituals, therefore, become the "time-markers" on the rhythmic cycle of seasons and life.

To the pre-literary society, the visible world is the result of a hierarchy of influences that are part of a spiritual, unseen world. In the order of most influential to the least influential, Newing notes the following. The first and foremost influence which permeates the universe is known as "mana." This spiritual power is the life force recognized as affecting everything. Although "mana" is not worshiped, divinities are thought to possess this force in highly concentrated forms. "Mana" is thought to concentrate itself in certain things with varying degree of intensity. One's position in the community depends upon his or her amount of "mana." The manipulation of this life force is the main function of tribal religious leaders. Second, the supreme being, usually considered a sky divinity, possesses more "mana" than any other spirit or human. He is more of a disinterested observer of human affairs, than a helper in time of need. Although this high god can be called upon for intervention, to bother him is to ask for trouble. Third, there are a multitude of divinities in addition to the supreme being. Each natural phenomenon is seen as expressions of that particular god. Fourth, good and evil spirits have access to the seen world. They dwell in all sorts of places, and people must be careful not to offend them. Evil spirits are able to take on various shapes and terrorize people. Good spirits watch and protect people's welfare. Fifth, ancestral spirits (or "the living dead") are thought to maintain a continuing relationship with families in the visible world. For this reason mortuary rites are of great importance. The soul must be completely severed from the deceased or it may return and cause harm to the family. Since death is almost always regarded as the result of witchcraft, another important factor in the mortuary rites is the determination of the source of witchcraft (37-41).

Both voodoo and Santeria come from this type of background. Although there are some similarities between voodoo and Santeria, they are distinct religions and will be considered as such in this chapter. To illustrate how these religions are from the same background yet different, the reader might compare them with Protestant denominationalism. For example, the Baptist Church and the Methodist Church both have their roots in the Protestant

Movement of the sixteenth century, yet they have each evolved into distinct religions. The same African pre-literary religion which evolved into voodoo in Haiti and Santeria in Cuba evolved into "candomble" in Brazil and "obea" in Jamaica.

WHAT IS VOODOO?

The term "voodoo" (also called "vodou," " vodun," or "hoodoo") derives from "vodu" which means "spirit" or "deity" in the Fon language of West Africa (Grolier). Those of Haitian background prefer to use the spelling "vodou" in order to "salute the historical roots of the religion and to convey its evolution from Africa to Haiti, but also to distance themselves from the general tendency of foreigners to devalue Haitian culture" (Galembo xxx). The spelling "voodoo" will be maintained in this chapter not to "devalue Haitian culture," but because it is the spelling with which most readers are familiar. The author has had personal friendships with many Haitians over the years, and he has developed great respect for them and their culture.

Voodoo was developed by African slaves brought to Haiti by French slave traders between the seventeenth and nineteenth centuries. White settlers and slave traders did not allow the Africans to practice their native religions. Instead, many Africans were "baptized" and forced to become Roman Catholics. However, Roman Catholicism was merely "superimposed on native rites and beliefs, which were still practiced in secret" by Africans (Settle Introduction). Therefore, voodoo is a "mixture of Roman Catholic ritual elements, which dates from the period of French colonization, and African theological and magical elements, which were brought to Haiti by slaves" formerly belonging to the people of West Africa (Britannica). Tribal deities, known as "loa," soon took on the form of Catholic saints. Voodoo worshipers considered the addition of these Catholic saints an enhancement to their religion. As voodoo evolved, it incorporated Catholic statues, candles, and relics into its rituals. "Voodooists do not regard this blending of the two faiths as profaning Christianity, but rather as enriching their voodoo cult" (Devillers 399). Like the religions of pre-literary societies, practitioners of voodoo profess a belief in a distant supreme being. However, the "effective divinities" are a plethora of spirits (Britannica). These spirits are called the "loa," which can be variously identified as local African gods, deified ancestors, or Roman Catholic saints (Britannica). In cultic practices of voodoo, a main goal is to manipulate these "loa" to accomplish either benevolent or malevolent purposes.

VOODOO CONCEPT OF HUMAN NATURE

According to voodoo, the human being is made up of five basic elements (adapted from Settle Death). First, the "corpse cadavre" is the mortal part of the human, consisting of the body, flesh, and blood. This is the only part of the human that decays after death. Second, the "n'âme" is the spirit that allows the body to function while it is alive. At death this spirit passes as energy into the soil. This part of the human is known as the "spirit of the flesh." Third, the "z'étoile" decides a persons destiny. This part of human nature resides in the heavens apart from the person's body. It is known as the "star of destiny," and is the least important part of human nature. The last two components, considered the most important, make up the human soul. The "gros-bon-ange" (literally, "great good angel") is the part of the soul that belongs to the vast pool of cosmic energy. At conception, part of the cosmic life force (cf. "mana" of pre-literary religions) passes into the human being. All living things are said to share in this cosmic life force so that all living things are connected to each other in a great web of energy. The "gros-bon-ange" is what keeps the body alive and able to experience feeling or sensation. After death it passes back into the great cosmic energy reservoir. Without the "gros-bon-ange," a person looses his or her life force. According to voodoo belief, a person's "gros-bon-ange" can be separated from him or her, and stored in a container where the energy can be used for other purposes. The "ti-bon-ange" (literally, "little good angel") makes up the other half of a person's soul. It is the source of personality. The "ti-bon-ange" represents the accumulation of a person's knowledge and experience, and is responsible for determining individual characteristics, personality, and will. The "ti-bon-ange" is the part of human nature that is most susceptible to sorcery. It can leave the body while dreaming, or when the body is possessed by the "loa."

VOODOO CONCEPT OF DEATH AND THE AFTERLIFE

According to voodoo, death is not the cessation of life. Although the "corps cadavre" decays and the "n'âme" which allowed the body to be animate returns to the earth as energy, the activities of life simply change from one condition to another. The soul, which consists of the "gros-bon-ange" and the "ti-bon-ange," endures after death. The "gros-bon-ange" is said to return to the high cosmic regions from which its energy was first drawn. In this celestial body of energy, it joins the other "loa" (deities) and becomes one of them. The "ti-bon-ange" is said to float around the body for a period of time before departing to the land of the dead. This departure must carefully be aided by rituals performed by a fully initiated priest or priestess.

The most important death ritual is to send the "gros-bon-ange" to the "cosmic community of ancestral spirits, where it will be worshiped by family members" as a divinity itself (Settle Death). If this ritual is not accomplished, the "gros-bon-ange" becomes trapped on earth and subsequently brings tragedy upon surviving family members. The "ti-bon-ange" must also be dealt with by a ritual called the "nine night," so named because the "ti-bon-ange" supposedly hoovers around the body for nine days. This ritual is performed to keep the "ti-bon-ange" in the grave. If this ritual is not performed, the "ti-bon-ange" may also wander the earth and bring harm upon others. As mentioned earlier, a fully initiated priest or priestess can separate the "ti-bon-ange" from the body. When this is done the "ti-bon-ange" is released to live in dark waters for a year and one day. After this period of time, the family ritually raises the "ti-bon-ange," now called an "espirit," and places it in a clay vessel where it is treated like a divinity.

Some cults within voodoo believe that everyone has evil within them. While this evil soul is in the body, it is controlled by the person's heart and brain. So long as the person is strong, this evil soul is kept in check. However, when the person dies, the evil soul is freed. Without the restraint of the deceased's heart and brain, this evil soul is capable of terrible harm upon the living. the "nine night" ritual is also used to ensure that this evil soul stays in the grave.

EVALUATING VOODOO CONCEPTS OF HUMAN NATURE AND AFTERLIFE

The voodoo concept of the afterlife is based upon many fundamental errors. First, the voodoo concept of the spiritual world is not in harmony with reality. While it is true that the spirit world revealed in the Bible involves much more than the average Christian realizes (cf. Rom. 8:38; Eph. 6:12), it is not the case that all things of creation house a "spiritual life force." There is an order of spiritual beings created by God (i.e. angels, Heb. 1:4-6), but humans are the only creatures of God who inhabit this world who are also spiritual in nature (cf. Eccles. 12:7; Acts 7:59). Second, the voodoo concept of human nature is false. The total teaching of the Bible reveals that humans consist, not of five parts, but of three parts; namely, body (the temporary housing for the everlasting spirit cf. 2 Cor. 4:16-5:1), soul (the life-ability which originates with God and which distinguishes the animate from the inanimate cf. Gen. 2:7), and spirit (the inner part of human beings that is eternal and which controls the mind and subsequent actions of all accountable people cf. Rom. 8:16). Although "soul" and "spirit" may be used interchangeably (cf. Matt. 10:28), there is a distinction between them (cf. Heb. 4:12; 1 Thess. 5:23). Third, the voodoo concept of human activity after death is false. Biblically speaking, physical death is the departure of the ever living human spirit from the temporal human body (John 19:30; Jas. 2:26). However, the human spirit does not return to any "cosmic energy reservoir," but is kept by God in his appointed place where it will be judged on the last day (cf. Luke 16:19-31; Heb. 9:27).

Much of voodoo belief involves the idea that spirits, both of the living and of the dead, can somehow be controlled by external manipulation. This control is said to extend into the seen and the unseen worlds. Although one can believe anything one desires (cf. 2 Thess. 2:8-12), Christians can take comfort in the fact that no power--internal, external, spiritual, or carnal--is stronger than the God whom they serve (cf. Ps. 66:7; Jer. 10:12; Rev. 4:11). Armed with "the weapons of our warfare," Christians can defeat every false way, including voodoo concepts of the afterlife (cf. 2 Cor. 10:3-6; Eph. 6:10-20).

WHAT IS SANTERIA?

"Santeria" is a term that is derived from a Spanish word for "saint" (santos), and it literally means, "the worship of saints." "Santeria" was first applied by the Spanish as a "pejorative term" to the "religious practices of the peasantry," who paid an "unusual amount of devotion and attention . . . to the Catholic Saints, often in preference to Jesus Christ" (Santeria). The term was again applied in Cuba to "identify the 'pagan' religion" (Santeria). The African people brought to Cuba as slaves where often referred to as "santos" (saints), because of the devotion they displayed toward their deities. This devotion was considered "the 'fanatical' worship of demigods and the neglect of 'God'" (Santeria). Thus, the term "Santeria" began as a demeaning designation to the religious practices and practitioners of African-Cuban slaves. In spite of its origin; however, the term has been accepted by practitioners of the religion in recent years.

BACKGROUND OF SANTERIA

Like voodoo, Santeria has its roots in Africa. According to Migene Gonzolez-Wippler, one of the most knowledgeable authorities this author researched, Santeria was "born in Nigeria, along the banks of the Niger River" among the inhabitants of that region known as the Yoruba people. These people once dwelt in the interior of West Africa, but due to invasions by other African tribes, the Yoruba people were forced to migrate to the Nigerian coast. It was here that they became vulnerable to slave traders (1). In order for the enslaved Yoruba people to keep their religion alive in the New World, their African religion had to undergo drastic changes.

It was in the New World that Santeria matured. "The changes that led to Santeria began in 1517, when Yoruba slaves had their first taste of Catholicism in Cuba" (Nunez 3). To be sure, the African gods were alive and well in the minds of the Africans as they were brought to the New World. Although African "liturgical seasons, prescribed rituals, traditional myths, and languages of worship were attenuated, replaced, and altered, or lost," most still remained, and "especially in Latin

America the gods lived on in the beliefs and rituals of the slaves' descendants" (Raboteau 16). The essence of the Yoruba religion survived by synthesizing itself with Catholicism, the religion of Cuba.

According to Gonzalez-Wippler, the African slaves in Cuba were "deeply influenced by the Catholic iconolatry of their Spanish masters." In order to hide their "magical and religious practices" from the Spaniards," they identified their deities with the saints of the Catholic Church" (3). In a somewhat satyrical way, Nunez illustrates this synthesis of African gods to Catholic saints as follows:

> "Elegera the playful messenger of the gods, cheerfully becomes the Holy Child of Atoch. Oshosi, the fierce god of war, shrugged his shoulders and became St. Norbert. Oshun, the hip-swinging goddess of those who know how to make love with skill and passion, became Our Lady of Charity . . . Chango, the invincible warrior chief, the whoring god of storm and lightening, showed his sense of humor. He turns into St. Barbara" (4).

Perhaps the epitome of this synthesis is observed by picture plate number sixty in Gonzalez-Wippler which shows Christ hanging on the cross surrounded by "The Seven African Powers." The pictures are those of Roman Catholic saints, but the name listed below each picture is that of a Santerian deity. What gives Santeria its particular "flavor" is its Cuban Catholic content. Even in the last decade of the twentieth century, "it is not unusual to enter a Catholic church in Cuba and see shrines to saints that you wouldn't see in Rome, and to see parishioners in trancelike states or reciting exotic prayers and incantations" (Williams 78).

The reason why many people have not heard of Santeria is explainable. Santeria is "not a religion of proselyters," but a "very private, mysterious faith" (Williams 79). According to Gonzalez-

Wippler, although the newly transported Africans were able to hide their deities "under the guise of Catholic saints," Spanish settlers began to realize what their slaves were doing. As a result, the Africans performed many of their "intricate system of rituals and ceremonies of a distinct magical nature" in the woods. Because these slaves received a great deal of persecution for practicing their religion, they were forced to "cloak their religion in secrecy." All the rituals, therefore, were conducted under "stringent vows of secrecy." These vows of secrecy became an inherent part of the Santeria tradition. The priests of Santeria are "adamant" about observing the vows of secrecy, even though in most places in the Caribbean and Americas secrecy is no longer necessary (3-4).

Santeria has no written standard of authority. Its traditions have been handed down orally for centuries. The written records that may be in existence are "either direct transcriptions from the oral tradition taken by interested researchers or from the notebooks in which a godmother or godfather laboriously wrote with a smeary pencil, awful grammar and spelling, the finer points to be remembered during the ceremonies" (Nunez 7). Because Santeria has no objective standard of authority, it is a very subjective religion, and even those who practice it cannot reasonably prescribe it as the only religion approved by God.

RELIGIOUS CONCEPTS OF SANTERIA

Like the ancient African (Yoruba) tradition, Santeria is based on the concepts of "ashé" and "ebbó." According to Gonzalez-Wippler, "ashé" (from a Yoruba word which literally means "so be it") is a word which represents divine power. It is the "power with which God Almighty–Oloddumare–created the universe." Everything in the universe consists of "ashé," and through "ashé" everything is possible. The deities (known as orishas) are the "repositories of Oloddumare's ashé." All of the "invocations, propitiations, spells, and rituals of Santeria are conducted to acquire ashé from the orishas." With the possession of ashé, "all problems can be solved, enemies can be subdued, love and money can be acquired." Ashé, therefore, is "authority" and "power of action." "Ebbó" is the "concept of sacrifice, the way in which the orishas are propitiated so that they will give us their ashé." (5).

In accord with the pre-literary religions examined earlier and similar to voodoo, central to the practice of Santeria is the role of dead ancestors. "Death looms in Santeria not as judgment or oblivion, torment or paradise, but as another kind of life that lives alongside of, and participates with, this one" (Ventura vii). Because the dead ancestors are still involved in their living relatives' lives, it is important that they be satisfied. According to Gonzalez-Wippler, the dead in one's family must be periodically fed with water, coffee, or bits of one's food. Before every ceremony, the dead in one's family must be honored (6).

The Santerian deities are known as "orishas." In most contexts the term "orisha" is used synonymously with the word "saint." According to Gonzalez-Wippler, Santeria worships a "central creative force, known as Oloddumare, who corresponds to the concept of God." According to her, "the orishas are not really gods, but the children and servants of Oloddumare." The orishas are not worshiped as gods, but as "guardian angels." Santeria believes that every person's life is "overseen by one of the orishas" (12-13). It does not matter whether one believes in the orishas or not, one has their protection and guidance throughout one's life. When a person chooses Santeria as his or her religion, "one of the first things he does is to ascertain who is his personal orisha" (Gonzalez-Wippler 13). When one learns of his or her particular orisha through one of the systems of divination, one must constantly petition that deity for help and guidance throughout one's life. In Santeria, "good and evil are not polar opposites, struggling in the figures of God and the Devil," but as with the Greek pantheon (which the orishas strikingly resemble), each orisha "is capable of doing good and evil" (Ventura vi). Although the number of African deities are thought to exceed six hundred, in Latin America the prominent orishas of Santeria are between twenty and twenty-five.

PRIESTS AND DIVINATIONS

In Santeria, there are no central figures (such as the pope or a cultic leader) who are considered central to the religion or who are worshipped in any way. The Santerian priests and priestesses are viewed as being "the mouthpieces of the orishas, or saints, and as the instructors in the mysteries of Santeria" (Gonzalez-Wippler 12). The main functions of the priest are to "honor the saints, obey them, interpret their commands for the faithful, and perform the rituals they demand" (Williams 79). The high priest of the religion (known as babalawo) is the only one who is allowed to offer blood sacrifices. The high priest also serves as a mediator between the priests or priestesses and the particular orisha they represent. When there are disputes among the priests or priestesses over which sacrifice or ritual their orisha desires, the high priest will confer the protocol.

Various divination systems are used by the priests and high priests to ascertain the will of the orishas. According to Gonzalez-Wippler, the priest uses "a set of sixteen cowrie shells to conduct his consultations with his clients." By means of these cowrie shells, "the santero [priest] can speak with the orishas and in this manner determine the best solutions for his client's problems." The high priest uses two forms of divination. The first form, known as the "opelé," involves a "long chain with eight equidistant medallions made of coconut rinds." The second form is only used during initiations and to determine who is the ruling orisha of an individual. This form is called the "Table of Ifá." It is "composed of a wooden tray upon which the babalawo [high priest] sprinkles a secret powder known as yefá." On this powder, the high priest "draws a series of vertical lines that he then interprets according to a series of versicles known as oddu" (17).

Both the priest and the high priest share the most common of the divination systems, known as "darle coco al santo." According to Gonzalez-Wippler, this divination system employs four pieces of coconut that are thrown on the floor to determine the desires of the orisha. The coconut is used "only to determine whether the orishas are pleased or displeased with a particular offer and how such an offer is to be disposed of" (17).

SACRIFICE RITUALS

Most rituals of Santeria involve some sort of sacrificial offering. Sacrifices may involve such things as coffee, flowers, fruit, and the burning of incense or candles. Santerian rituals involve the entire community of practitioners. According to Ventura, "nothing important can take place without drummers and people willing to cook the food, prepare the place, and participate." Even an initiation ritual, which focuses on one person, "requires a community to properly meet and honor and give their bodies to the Orishas" (vii). The type of sacrifice that is to be offered depends on the particular orisha and the reason for the sacrifice. The priest must ascertain what the orisha desires, usually through the cowrie shell system of divination.

Animal sacrifices are reserved only for two occasions. First, animal sacrifices are called for "in major situations such as sickness or serious misfortune" (Sacrifice). Santeria considers blood as "the essence of life," and it must not, therefore, "be shed lightly" (Gonzalez-Wippler 5). An orisha may request an animal, usually a chicken or a dove, in order for the orisha to come to the aid of a person (Sacrifice). Since blood sacrifices are "never [to be] offered indiscriminately or whimsically," this blood sacrificing ritual is reserved for occasions where "great forces are invariably in play, and often the life of a person is in danger or a major undertaking is involved" (Gonzalez-Wippler 5-6).

Second, animal sacrifices are called for during initiation rituals. "Initiation" may be for an individual who decides to become a practitioner of Santeria, or for a practitioner who becomes a priest. Initiation is referred to as a "birthing process," and, according to Santeria, "in every birth there is blood" (Sacrifice). According to Nunez, animal sacrifices for initiation rituals involve the following specifics. Only a high priest may kill the sacrificial animal. All animals to be used must be "healthy, beautiful, and fat." The orishas must be fed, and it is blood which gives strength to both the orisha and the one being initiated. The animals are kept outside of the room where the altar is located until the very moment of their sacrifice. Four legged animals are offered first, followed by the birds (usually chickens) when required. The animals are covered with colored cloths which indicate the orisha to whom they belong. The initiate must touch and rub the animal with various parts of his or her body, including sexual organs. The animal's legs are tied together by the high priest, and it is placed on the floor, usually on a bed of leaves. The animal's neck is stretched, and its jugular vein is cut by the high priest. The blood is collected in a container to be fed to the orisha. The initiate will also drink the animal's blood, sometimes directly from the spewing neck stump (19-26).

EVALUATION OF SANTERIA CONCEPTS AND PRACTICES

First, consider the Santeria concept of "ashé." This power, through which the Almighty created all things, is said to permeate everything (cf. the "mana" of pre-literary societies). Thus, such things as the rocks, trees, and dirt are believed to have divine power in them. However, according to the Bible, the only true, objective standard of religious authority, only God has divine power (Gen. 17:1; Rev. 11:17). This fact is made clear in that only God can create life (Gen. 1-2). Humans, made in the image of God, are the only representatives of God among the entire created world (cf. Gen. 1:26-27; 9:6; Jas. 3:9). This, of course, does not mean that humans possess any kind of divine power, for only God possess that. Christians, however, are spiritually empowered by God through obedience to His word to carry out His will (cf. Phil. 4:13).

Second, the "orishas" of Santeria are nothing more than resurrected pagan gods renamed. They are not considered to be perfect in their attributes. They have "human qualities and needs" (Williams 79). According to Ventura, "one cannot be better than the gods, and if the gods are destructive and irrational at times that doesn't mean they're 'evil'; it means that destructive and irrational things happen in life." He says that these "destructive and irrational" happenings are to "be lived with, guarded against, fought, healed, forgiven, understood, and remembered, but not stigmatized as coming from the source of all darkness" (vii). On face value, it is difficult to understand why any one would rely upon such unreliable gods. Such a system, however, seems to have built-in excuses to justify whatever behavior a practitioner may desire. If one lies, cheats, steals, or fornicates, one can blame it on one's orisha. The God of the Bible, however, is perfect in His attributes. God is completely holy, and He calls upon all His followers to imitate His holiness (Lev. 11:44). Though humans are weak through the flesh (Matt. 26:41), their failure is not due to God, but to their own sinfulness (cf. Jas. 1:12-15).

Third, the Santeria systems of divination are nothing more than the deceptiveness of Satan in action. There is absolutely no foretelling power in cowrie shells or coconut rinds, nor does any divine personality communicate through such objects. To those who do not love the truth, God will send "strong delusion, that they should believe a lie: That they all might be damned who believe not the truth, but had pleasure in unrighteousness" (2 Thess. 2:10-12). Those who practice and/or believe in such systems of divination are simply people who are deceived. Even if what the priest says through the cowrie shells comes true, the success of his prediction is not the standard by which he is deemed legitimate. The standard which determines whether the priest is truly from God is the message that he teaches (cf. Deut. 13:1-4). If the priest teaches what God teaches in His written revelation, he is a true spokesman of God. If the priest teaches that which is contrary to God's written revelation, he is a false priest.

Fourth, Santeria's sacrifices, especially the blood sacrifices, are displeasing to God. One reason for the sacrifices of Santeria is that "it is not enough to ask the gods to bless us. We must bless them as well and find a way to bless their world" (Ventura x). The gods of Santeria, therefore, rely upon the sacrifices of their human followers for their own well being. Again, this is quite a contrast with the only true God. The blood sacrifices are a part of the old pagan tradition that has been carried over. Practitioners of Santeria will claim that animal sacrifices have been a part of religious ritual throughout human history, and that their offering of blood should not be considered grotesque or disrespectful. Several sources claim that Santeria respects life more than slaughter houses and those who thoughtlessly eat meat (Sacrifice; Ventura viii; et al.). Blood sacrifice disregards the "once and for all time sacrifice" of Christ (cf. Heb. 9:24-26). Of course, the practitioner of Santeria does not respect the Christ or the God of the Bible. The ritual that accompanies blood sacrifices is hideous to the Lord. While it is true that the Israelites of old were to offer animal sacrifices to the Lord (cf. Lev. 4-5; 16 et al.), they were never to drink the blood (Lev. 17:10-14), nor to accompany the sacrifice with lascivious acts. If they have not already reached this point, people who participate in these rituals must surely be on the verge of being "given up" by God (cf. Rom. 1:21-32).

Santeria is a "religion of trance, mystery, possession, blood, and sex" (Nunez 1). Santeria is a false religion, opposed to God, but attractive to many people who wish to legitimize worldly lust and hold to African tradition. "The basic difference between the Yoruba priest and the santero is that the latter practices his magic in the asphalt jungles of the big cities instead of the African wilderness . . . Santeria is jungle magic adapted to city living" (Gonzalez-Wippler 18). Faithful children of God, particularly those who work in Latin-Caribbean countries, must be aware of Santeria in order to better reach these people with the Gospel. Even against Santeria, Christians must remember that "the weapons of our warfare are not carnal, but mighty through God to the pulling down of strong holds; casting down imaginations, and every high thing that exalteth itself against the knowledge of God, and bringing into captivity every thought to the obedience of Christ." (2 Cor. 10:4-5).

WORKS CITED

Beckwith, Carol and Angela Fisher. "The African Roots of Voodoo." National Geographic, August 1995:101-113.

Brooks, Richard M. "Jury Convicts Mortician of Abusing Corpse." The Ledger 6 March 1999: B7.

Devillers, Carole. "Haiti's Voodoo Pilgrimages: Of Spirits and Saints." National Geographic, March 1985: 395-408.

Encyclopedia Britannica, 1996 electronic version.

Galembo, Phyllis. Vodou: Visions and Voices of Haiti. Berkeley, CA: Ten Speed Press, 1998.

Gonzalez-Wippler, Migene. Santeria: The Religion. St. Paul, MN: Llewellyn Publications, 1996.

Grolier Multimedia Encyclopedia, 1997 edition.

Newing, Edward G. "Religions of Pre-Literary Societies." The World's Religions. 4th rev. ed. Ed. Norman Anderson. Grand Rapids: Eerdmans, 1975.

Nunez, Luis Manuel. Santeria: A Practical Guide to Afro-Caribbean Magic. Dallas, TX: Spring Publications, 1992.

Raboteau, Albert J. Slave Religions: The "Invisible Institution" in the Antebellum South. New York: Oxford University Press, 1978.

Sacrifice. Internet. 15 March 1999. Available www.seanet.com/~efunmoyiwa/sacrif.htm.

Santeria, La Regla Lucumi, Lukumi, Etc. Internet. 15 March 1999. Available. www.religioustolerance.org/santeri.htm

Settle, Shannon Turlington. Introduction to Vodun. Internet. 15 March 1999. Available www.arcana.com/shannon/voodoo/intro.htm

- - - Vodun and Death. Internet. 15 March 1999. Available www.arcana.com/ shannon/voodoo/death.htm.

Williams, Stephen. Cuba: The Land, the History, the People, the Culture. New York: Friedman Publishing, 1994.

Ventura, Michael. Forward. Santeria: A Practical Guide to Afro-Caribbean Magic. By Luis Manuel Nunez. Dallas, TX: Spring Publications, 1992: v-x.

Chapter 10

The State of The Dead

Denny Petrillo

The question concerning what happens to one after death is often asked, because it is a matter that concerns all of us. However, it is not a question that is easily answered. The reason for this is because there is no one Scripture that will answer the question. We must combine several passages to completely understand both death itself and what happens after death. However, it *is* possible to understand. The Bible student will simply be challenged to consider all the evidence God gives in His word.

A fairly recent survey demonstrated some rather interesting perspectives on religion and life after death. Whereas interest in religion is declining worldwide, including the United States, nearly 80% of Americans believe in life after death. And, interestingly enough, this percentage has remained unchanged for two decades. Overall by religious groups, 84% of Protestants, 76% of Catholics and 31% of Jews said they believe in life after death (Briggs 8). Also, in a November 1990 Gallup survey, 78% of the respondents said they believe there is a heaven (where good people will be rewarded) and 60% said they believed there was a hell (where bad people will be punished).

It is clear, then, that a great deal of interest remains in the topic of life after death. And, while many people believe that *something* must surely happen beyond this life, their understanding of just what that might be is somewhat vague.

What has, to some degree, compounded the problem is the misinformation being given by various religious groups today. There are religions that maintain that when one dies he or she no longer exists (The Watchtower 4-6). While this might be expected to come from atheists, it is difficult to understand from those who say their teachings are based on the Bible.

In this study we will address the following questions: (1) Why do people die? (2) What is death? (3) What happens to the body at death? (4) What happens to people when they die? (5) Is there a 'waiting place' for the dead until the Second Coming of Christ?

WHY DO PEOPLE DIE?

By looking both at the Biblical record as well as biological evidence, it seems clear that mankind became familiar with death by looking at the animal and vegetable worlds. Many animals exist by eating other animals, and plants often receive important nutrients by the decomposing of dead trees and plants. So it seems certain that Adam and Eve would have had some conception of death when God first said:

> And the Lord God commanded the man, saying, 'From any tree of the garden you may eat freely; but from the tree of the knowledge of good and evil you shall not eat, for in the day that you eat from it you shall surely die (Genesis 2:16-17).

This passage includes the first time the word "death" occurs. This passage would also indicate the first time that Adam and Eve would be made aware that *they themselves* could die. Whereas they saw death in the plant and animal kingdoms, it was not a consideration in the real of mankind. Notice also that God makes a connection between **death** and **sin**. If Adam and Eve had kept themselves from eating the forbidden fruit they would not have died. Instead, they would have had continual access to the "tree of life" and "live forever" (Genesis 3:22).

WHAT IS DEATH?

Since the Biblical record clearly connects death with the sinfulness of man, it might be asked "what *kind* of death" is God referring to? Those who ask this question note that God said "*the day* you eat you shall die," but Adam did not die on that day. As a matter of fact, he lived to be 930 years old (Genesis 5:5). Many scholars believe that number represents how long Adam lived <u>after</u> he was removed from the garden. So, based on this evidence, it is suggested that God was not referring to **physical death** but **spiritual death**. Here are the basic arguments offered for the various positions:

1) Physical death is what is meant, but God suspended the execution of death by extending grace to Adam and Eve.

2) Physical death is what is meant, but the phrase "in the day you eat of it" is a Hebrew idiom meaning "as surely as you eat of it" you shall die. The same phrase is found in 1 Kings 2:37 and Exodus 10:28 and the phrase "in the day" seems to mean "as surely as" (Hoekema 81).

> "Understanding the expression in the same sense in Genesis 2:17, therefore, we conclude that it does not need to mean "on the particular day that you eat this fruit you shall die," but rather, "as surely as you eat this fruit you shall die." On the basis of this interpretation, further, the fact that Adam and Eve did not die physically on the same day that they ate from the forbidden tree need not cause us any particular difficulty" (Hoekema 81-82).

3) Physical death is what is meant, but God's words should be understood as "on the day you eat you shall *begin* to die."

4) Spiritual death is what is meant, where death represents a separation from God. Thus, when Adam and Eve were sent from the garden they no longer enjoyed the daily presence of God who "walked in the garden" (Genesis 3:8).

5) A combination of spiritual death and physical death is meant. This position seems to have the most merit because of the following points. *First*, man was created as both a physical and a spiritual being. Thus death would logically effect both of these aspects of man. *Second*, "according to Scripture the deepest meaning of life is fellowship with God, the deepest meaning of death must be separation from God" (Hoekema 82). *Third*, the Scriptures seem to attach both a physical and a spiritual consequence to what happened in the garden. In Genesis 3:19 God clearly connects the sin with physical death. Note God's words: "By the sweat of your face you shall eat bread, Till you return to the ground, Because from it you were taken; For you are dust, And to dust you shall return."

In addition to this passage there is Genesis 3:22-23 where God commands that Adam and Eve be removed from the garden, lest they eat from the tree of life and "live forever." The only logical meaning of this passage is physical death. In 1 Corinthians 15 Paul is making an extended argument in behalf of the resurrection of Christ and also the resurrection of believers. In making his argument he refers back to the garden. Note his words:

> "But now Christ has been raised from the dead, the first fruits of those who are asleep. For since by a man came death, by a man also came the resurrection of the dead. For as in Adam all die, so also in Christ all shall be made alive. But each in his own order: Christ the first fruits, after that

> those who are Christ's at His coming..." (1 Corinthians 15:20-24).

Yet in Romans 5:12-21 Paul, again alluding back to what happened in the garden, maintains that "through one man sin entered into the world, and death through sin, and so death spread to all men, because all sinned...." It seems clear that Paul has *spiritual* death in mind because of the following reasons: (a) his other references to "death" are spiritual in application, not physical (6:2,4,7,8,11,23, etc.); (b) Paul says that death came to all men "because all sinned." If physical death is what is meant, then one would not be subject to death until he or she sins. However, infants die even though they are free from sin; (c) Paul's point is that one is *spiritually* separated from God when he or she sins (going back to 3:10-23), which is why all need to be "reconciled" (Romans 5:11; cf. Isaiah 59:1,2); (d) It is difficult to explain exactly the point Paul is trying to make by saying all die physically because of Adam. Of what value is this information? How does it fit with what has been said, or what he is going to say? However, it is clear what point is being made if spiritual death is meant.

In Ephesians 2:1-2 Paul argues that sinful man lives in a state of spiritual death: "For you were dead in your trespasses and sins" is a statement made to those who are obviously alive physically. He then goes on to say that God, "even when we were dead in our transgressions, made us alive together with Christ..." (2:5). In Romans 8:10 Paul maintains that "...though the body is dead because of sin, yet the spirit is alive because of righteousness."

What then is the answer to the first question: "why do people die?" The answer is sin. And the answer to the second question "what is death?" is, simply stated, a separation. It involves a separation of the body from the spirit (physical death) and a separation of man and God (spiritual death). If it were not because of sin people would die neither spiritually or physically. Note the words of Leon Morris:

> "When man sinned he passed into a new state, one dominated by, and at the same time symbolized by, death. It is likely that spiritual death and physical death are not being thought of as separate, so that the one involves the other" (10).

Anthony Hoekema also adds:

> "In other words, after man had sinned, he died immediately in the spiritual sense, and therefore became subject to what we call eternal death - eternal separation from the loving presence of God. At the same time man entered into a state in which bodily death was now inevitable" (82).

WHAT HAPPENS TO THE BODY AT DEATH?

While spiritual death was discussed briefly above, it is now our desire to consider what the Bible teaches about *physical* death. Ever since Cain took the life of Abel man has had to deal with the painful reality of death. Indeed the Bible teaches that all will die (Hebrews 9:27) except for those who are alive when Jesus returns (1 Thessalonians 4:11-18).

The Bible has many phrases to describe death (from Lewis 176): Death is "to go the way of all the earth" (Joshua 23:14; 1 Kings 2:2); "to be gathered to one's people" (Genesis 15:15; 25:8; 35:29,33; Numbers 20:24,26; 31:2; Deuteronomy 32:50); "to sleep with one's fathers" (1 Kings 2:10; 11:21; 2 Kings 20:21); or to go to one's "eternal home" (Ecclesiastes 12:5).

God designed the body to immediately begin decomposing at death. He said to Adam: "for you are dust, and to dust you shall return" (Genesis 3:19; cf. 2:7; Psalm 90:3; 104:29; Ecclesiastes 12:7).

But the Bible also makes it clear that a separation between the body and the spirit occurs at death. Ecclesiastes 12:7 states: "then the dust will return to the earth as it was, and the spirit will return to God who gave it." The Hebrew also seems to have a word that represents one's "life force" (*nephesh)*, which leaves the body upon death (Genesis 35:18; Jonah 4:3), but is present when one lives (Genesis 1:20, 24, 30; 2:7; 9:12, 15-17). Even animals are described in this way, so that when their *nephesh* is removed, they die (Psalm 104:29). The medical world has long been mystified about the literal difference between one who lives and one who is dead. For example, on the operating table the doctors work to keep one alive. But, as sometimes happens, the person dies. What physically is different? Is he suddenly missing some organs? Did the brain lose some of its mass? No, physically there is no difference. All the same parts remain, but for some reason the person no longer lives. The Bible explains this phenomenon as one's "spirit" (*nephesh*) leaving the body. This is the "life force" that God gave all living things. And, as God gave that life force/spirit (Genesis 2:7) that life force/spirit returns to God upon one's death (Ecclesiastes 12:7). There are some passages in which the "spirit" (*nephesh)* represents the person himself (Deuteronomy 6:5; 23:24; Judges 16:30; Psalm 107:9; Daniel 7:15).

The New Testament seems to have two words to share this concept. James 2:26 notes that the body apart from the spirit (*pneuma*) is dead, and Luke 8:55 has the spirit leaving Jairus' daughter when she died, and returning to her when Jesus brought her to life. Other passages equally indicate the spirit (*pneuma*) to represent this "life force" (Matthew 27:50; Luke 23:46; 1 Peter 3:18; Acts 7:59). A second word, *psuche,* often indicates a similar concept (Matthew 2:20; 20:28; Luke 12:16-20; Acts 5:5, 10; 12:23; 20:10). There are passages, however, where *psuche* indicates more that just a life force.

For example, Jesus says not to fear those who can kill just the body, but rather to fear Him who is able to destroy both the soul (*psuche)* and the body in hell (Matthew 10:28; cf. Mark 8:36,37).

WHAT HAPPENS TO PEOPLE WHEN THEY DIE?

As mentioned in the introduction, there are those who maintain that death brings a complete end to a person's existence. Apparently there were even some in the New Testament who destroyed other's faiths by such a doctrine (2 Timothy 2:18; cf. 1 Corinthians 15:12ff). However, the Bible does clearly teach the "immortality of the soul" (the idea that after physical death some aspect of the person lives on).

Two words are frequently translated "immortality" in the English Bible: *athanasia* and *aphtharsia.* In 1 Corinthians 15:53-54 Paul says:

> "For this perishable must put on the imperishable (*aphtharsia*); and this mortal must put on immortality (*athanasia*). But when this perishable will have put on the imperishable *(aphtharsia)* and this mortal will have put on immortality (*athanasia*), then will come about the saying that is written, 'Death is swallowed up in victory.'"

There are a few passages in which the word *aphtharsia* is used. Paul says that those who persevere in doing good "seek for glory and honor and immortality, eternal life" (Romans 2:7). He mentions that it was Jesus who brought "life and immortality" to light through the Gospel (2 Timothy 1:10). Other passages equally tie in the concept of an eternal/immortal aspect to all people (1 Corinthians 9:52; 15:52; 1 Peter 1:4, 23; 3:4).

One might observe that this is a surprisingly small number of passages, considering the magnitude of this topic. However, the Bible (more specifically the New Testament) emphasizes not so much the existence of people after death but rather the *quality* of that existence. In other words, it is *assumed* that we will live on. The more important question is what will life be like beyond this one. Will it be pleasant and beautiful? Will it be filled with pain and torment? Will it be neither, but just a colorless, emotionless existence?

Before those questions can be answered, however, another one must be addressed first. Since the Bible teaches that the dead will live on, **where** will they live? While one might think that the answer to this question would also answer the question regarding the quality of life, such is not the case.

In the Old Testament when a person dies he goes to a place called *Sheol*. This word occurs 66 times in the Hebrew scriptures and signifies the dark (Job 10:21f) "realm of the dead" which is located beneath the earth (Genesis 37:35; 42:38; Job 26:5; Isaiah 14:11, 15; Ezekiel 31:15). While several passages indicate a connection with Sheol and the grave, the two are not always synonymous. It seems better to understand Sheol as referring to the "realm of the dead" (Jeremias 1:146). "Sheol is the Old Testament manner of asserting that death does not terminate human existence" (Ladd 194).

When the Septuagint translators needed to translate into Greek the Hebrew word *Sheol* they always used *Hades*. The word *Hades* occurs only 10 times in the Greek New Testament. The word comes from the Greek *idein* - "to see" thereby meaning "the unseen realm" (Lewis 182; Bauer 16-17). There are no passages in the New Testament which dramatically change our understanding from the Old Testament study of *Sheol*. By studying the words *Sheol/Hades* one can make the following observations:

1) *Sheol/Hades is a place to which all go, regardless of whether they were righteous or unrighteous.* Job said it is the "house of meeting for all living" (30:23), and is a place that never says "enough"

(Proverbs 30:16). The evil Korah and his followers were swallowed by the earth and sent to Sheol (Numbers 16:30,31), and the Psalmist says concerning the wicked, "As sheep they are appointed for Sheol...and their form shall be for Sheol to consume" (Psalm 49:14). Yet the righteous Jacob recognized that he would go down to Sheol (Genesis 37:35), and the Psalmist wrote: "For thou wilt not abandon my soul to Sheol, Neither wilt Thou allow Thy Holy One to see the pit" (Psalm 16:10). While perhaps seeing an application for himself, the Psalmist was also making a prophecy that would later be applied to the resurrection of Christ (Acts 2:27,31), indicating that Jesus Himself went to Sheol when He died.

2) *Sheol/Hades is a place where its inhabitants are no longer aware of earthly events.* Solomon states that "the living know they will die; but the dead do not know anything, nor have they any longer a reward, for their memory is forgotten. Indeed their love, their hate, and their zeal have already perished, and they will not longer have a share in all that is done under the sun" (Ecclesiastes 9:5-6). So while the dead will have a memory of circumstances on the earth (Luke 16:27-28) they will have no knowledge of events taking place after they died.

3) *Sheol/Hades is a place where there are no longer opportunities to change one's eternal destiny.* In Sheol man cannot praise God (Isaiah 38:18; Psalm 6:5; 30:9; 88:10-12; 115:17) perhaps in a hope to change what they know will be their eternal destiny (Isaiah 38:18; Psalm 88:10-12). Solomon perhaps gives the best overall description of Sheol: "Whatever your hand finds to do, verily, do it with all your might; for there is no activity or planning or wisdom in Sheol where you are going" (Ecclesiastes 9:10). The rich man in Luke 16 recognizes that there is nothing that can happen to bring him any change of location or any comfort.

4) *Sheol/Hades is a place where its inhabitants are conscious.* In perhaps the clearest passage, the rich man of Luke 16 is aware of his own pain, the presence of Lazarus and Abraham, and a memory of his brothers back home. David knew that even in Sheol he would recognize the presence of God (Psalm 139:8). The inhabitants of Sheol are called "shades" or weak ones (Job 26:5; Proverbs 2:18; 21:16; Psalm 88:10; Isaiah 14:9; 26:14). In Revelation 6:9-11 the "souls under the altar" who had been martyred for the Gospel were aware that their shed blood had not been avenged.

5) *Sheol/Hades is a place of no return.* Job observed that "he who goes down to Sheol does not come up. He will not return again to his house" (Job 7:9-10; cf. 10:21; 16:22; 20:9). Once a person dies, he will not return to earth either as himself, someone else, or even an animal or insect (the doctrine of reincarnation). Hebrews 9:27 affirms that after death one will face the judgement. 1 Thessalonians 4:11ff states that when one dies he "rests" until Jesus comes. The rich man in Luke 16 is offered no hope of returning to earth to make amends for his evil deeds.

IS THERE A 'WAITING PLACE' FOR THE DEAD UNTIL THE SECOND COMING OF CHRIST?

There is considerable discussion regarding this question. While few will dispute that all the dead, both righteous and wicked, go to Sheol or Hades (understood simply as the "realm of the dead" without a distinction between the righteous and the wicked), there are basically two positions regarding Sheol and Hades. These positions are, simply stated, as follows:

1) There is an "intermediate state," which is divided into two sections. One, called "Paradise" or "Abraham's bosom" is where the righteous dead reside awaiting the final judgment; and the other, called

"torment" is where the unrighteous dead reside awaiting the final judgment. When this final judgment takes place all the dead will be sent to either heaven or hell.

2) The dead go directly to their eternal home - either heaven or hell.

While there are points of merit for both positions, the Biblical evidence seems to point more clearly to the first one; that there is a 'waiting place' for both the righteous and the wicked. Consider the following arguments:

First, while the dead go to Hades, Hades never designates the place of final punishment of the wicked. The eternal dwelling of the wicked is called *geenna* or "hell" (Lewis 186).

Second, in the New Testament Hades clearly serves an interim purpose, receiving the souls at death (Luke 16:23) and yielding them up at the resurrection (Revelation 20:13) (Lewis 186).

Third, Jesus' teaching in Luke 16:19-31 is the clearest description of what happens immediately after death. Lazarus is not said to go to "heaven" but instead to "Abraham's bosom." Equally, the rich man is not said to be in hell, but "in Hades he lifted up his eyes, being in torment" (16:23). Lewis notes, "The judgment has not yet taken place; he is not in hell" (188). Hoekema says,

> "It should further be noted that the parable does not picture conditions as they will be after the resurrection. In verses 27-28 the rich man refers to his five brothers who are still living on the earth - this situation would be impossible if the resurrection had already occurred (cf. also v. 31). We conclude, then, that both the sufferings associated with hades and the comforts associated with Abraham's bosom, as described in this parable, occur in the intermediate state" (101).

Fourth, in 2 Peter 2:9 Peter writes: "The Lord knows how to rescue the godly from temptation, and to keep the unrighteous under punishment for the day of judgment." He had earlier said that God has cast sinning angels into hell and committed them to pits of darkness, "reserved for judgment" (v. 4). Both of these passages indicate a temporary judgment which takes place before a final judgment. The phrase "for the day of judgment" in verse 10 is *eis hemeran kriseos* and could be translated "until" the day of judgment, showing that the punishment being given now is not the final punishment, but a punishment which takes place before the judgment day (cf. Jeremias 148; Boettner 91ff). Regarding this passage Hoekema concludes:

> "This passage, therefore, confirms what we have learned from the Parable of the Rich Man and Lazarus, and tells us that the ungodly undergo continuing punishment (the nature of which is here not further described) between their death and the Day of Judgment" (102).

Fifth, in Luke 23:43 Jesus spoke of the thief of going with him to "Paradise" - not to heaven. He says that "today you shall be with me in Paradise." "The obvious antithesis in the passage is between the indefinite 'when you come in your kingdom' used by the thief, and 'today you shall be with me' used by Jesus" (Lewis 189). The word "Paradise" is used in Jewish writings to refer to a location on earth, sometimes a location in heaven, and sometimes a location between heaven and earth (4 Ezra 7:36, 123; 8:52; 2 Baruch 51:10-11; 2 Enoch 8:1ff). This being the case, it cannot be said with any certainty that the use of the word in the New Testament always refers to the same place. For example, when Paul was caught up into Paradise (2 Corinthians 12:3), was he referring to the same place that Jesus spoke of to the thief? Lewis notes:

> "Many contend that it is; but this position faces the difficulty that according to Acts 2:27,31, Jesus went to Hades at death rather than to heaven. Because of this difficulty, from the chain of evidence we have presented, we deduce the idea that Paradise in Jesus' statement is a designation for a part of hades. We then connect Paradise wit the parable to deduce that this is where Abraham and Lazarus must be. That it was not heaven also follows from the fact that after three days in Hades Jesus said to the woman, 'Touch me not for I have not yet ascended to my Father' (John 20:17). God's dwelling obviously is in heaven (2 Chron. 6:33). Jesus had not gone to heaven; Hades in the Lukan passage is not in heaven; Paradise in the thief passage is not in heaven" (190-91).

Sixth, Jesus promised to go and prepare a place for His disciples, a place that they would be able to enjoy when He "comes again" (John 14:1-3). It seems clear from Jesus' statement that this heavenly abode in His "father's house" will not be enjoyed until after the second coming of Christ.

Seventh, Paul did not believe he would receive the "crown of life" until the day of judgment (2 Timothy 4:8). This concurs with Jesus' statement that men would receive their reward "at the resurrection of the just" (Luke 14:12-14) and at the hour when all who are in the tombs hear His voice and come forth (John 5:28-29).

Eighth, it does not seem logical that God would send people to their eternal dwelling, only to call them back for a universal judgment (Matthew 25:31-33), and then resend them to where they were originally. What purpose would that judgment serve? Whereas the view of an intermediate state provides a logical explanation for the final judgment. The final judgment is not for the purpose of letting people know whether they will be saved or lost - they already knew that as soon as they died. The final judgment is for the issuing of eternal rewards and punishments, and for explaining why people were given the judgment they were given (Matthew 25:34-46; cf. Revelation 20:11-14).

CONCLUSION

In conclusion it would be worthwhile to note that the Bible describes *four conditions* or states one will be in at the time of his or her death. There are no other conditions.

(1) **One dies as an infant**. We are all born into the world pure - without sin. Although some teach that we are born with sin, this is not a Biblical doctrine (see Ezekiel 18:20). If the infant dies before he is old enough to know and understand sin he/she will go directly to paradise (Matthew 18:1-6)

(2) **One dies never having obeyed the Bible**. When the child grows up, he learns of sin and commits sin, thus separating himself from God (Romans. 3:23; Isaiah 59:1,2). He becomes worldly, committing sins (such as lying, stealing, etc.). If he never repents of that sin he will, like the rich man in Luke 16, go to torment when he dies.

(3) **One dies after having obeyed the Gospel of Christ and remained faithful to it.** Jesus came and died so that we can be forgiven of those sins we commit. The way we have our sins forgiven is by the "new birth" (John 3:3-5) - that is, by baptism. The process by which we obtain forgiveness is illustrated as follows:. First people must **hear** the Gospel. We cannot learn and obey Jesus until we hear of Him (Romans 10:14-17). Second, people must **believe in Jesus**. We learn of Jesus, then we believe in Him (Mark 16:16; Romans 10:9,10). Third, people must **repent**. Repentance means to "stop

doing wrong - start doing right." When we learn of Jesus we find that He wants us to turn away from our sins (Luke 13:3,5; Acts 17:30,31). Fourth, people must **confess** Jesus as Lord. This is where we let others know that we plan to follow Jesus (Romans 10:9-10). Fifth, people must be **baptized**. This is, according to the Bible, immersion in water (Romans 6:3-4; Acts 8:38; 22:16; Mark 16:15-16; Galatians 3:27; 1 Peter 3:21). Without following the Bible's instructions, we cannot be saved - or enter into Christ's church (or kingdom). When one dies a part of Christ's church, a faithful Christian, he goes to Paradise. Jesus calls this Paradise "Abraham's Bosom." It is called this to symbolize a place of comfort and peace

(4) **One dies after obeying, then becoming unfaithful.** There are some who have been saved at one time in their life (that is, were in Christ's church) and then fall away from Christ (Galatians 5:4; 2 Peter 2:20-22). If they die in this state of unfaithfulness they also go to Torment.

There are no other conditions in which one might die. Thus all who have died since the creation of the world will be described by one of these four conditions. Jesus also teaches that there is no way a person can change the place they are in (Luke 16:26). Therefore, people will know as soon as they die whether they are saved or lost, and at that point there is nothing they can do to change their destiny (that is why it is so important to obey in this life! 2 Corinthians 5:10).

Also, it is our body which goes to the grave, whereas our spirit goes to either Paradise or Torment, depending on how we've lived (see Luke 8:49-56, especially verse 55).

The entire place that includes Paradise and Torment is called "Hades." This is not the same place as Hell. Even Jesus, when he died and was buried went to Hades (Acts 2:27).

Then, on a day that God has selected, all will come to Him and stand in judgment (2 Corinthians 5:10; Acts 17:30-31). There will be some who have not died yet, and many who have (1 Thess. 4:13-18). All will be raised from the grave together (John 5:28-29), and there will be a uniting of the spirit of man with his body. However, this body will now be imperishable and immortal (1 Corinthians 15:50-58). On this day of judgment, Jesus will separate the faithful (sheep) and send them to Heaven and send the unfaithful (goats) to Hell (Matthew 25:31-46).

WORKS CITED

Bauer, Walter. A Greek-English Lexicon of the New Testament and Other Early Christian Literature. Second edition. Translated and edited by William F. Arndt, F. Wilbur Gingrich and Frederick W. Danker. Chicago: The University of Chicago Press, 1979.

Boettner, Loraine. Immortality. Philadelphia: The Presbyterian and Reformed Publishing Co., 1975.Briggs, David. "Most Americans Still Believe in Afterlife." Rocky Mountain News (Denver): January 19, 1993.

Hoekema, Anthony A. The Bible and the Future. Grand Rapids: Eerdmans Publishing Co., 1979.

Jeremias, Joachim. "*Hades*." In Theological Dictionary of the New Testament, 1:146-49. Edited by Gerhard Kittel. Translated by Geoffrey W. Bromiley. Grand Rapids: Eerdmans Publishing Co., 1964.

Ladd, George Eldon. A Theology of the New Testament. Grand Rapids: Eerdmans Publishing Co., 1974.

Lewis, Jack P. "The Intermediate State of the Dead." Exegesis of Difficult Passages. Searcy, Arkansas: Resource Publications, 1988.

Major, Trevor J. "Does the Soul Survive Death?" Reasoning from Revelation 2.10 (October, 1990):1-2.

Morris, Leon. The Wages of Sin. London: Tyndale Publishing House, 1955.

Smith, Wilbur M. The Biblical Doctrine of Heaven. Chicago: Moody Press, 1968.

The Watchtower. The Watchtower Society, Brooklyn, NY: 9/1/90:4-6.

Chapter 11

Mediums & Channeling

Darrell Conley

In recent years there has been an upsurge of interest in what is sometimes called "mediumship," but is more often known as "channeling." This is the pretense to be in touch with the "spirit world," most particularly with some departed loved one, either directly or through some "spirit entity." It is incredible that in this age of unbelief, when supposedly the majority of people are so materialistic and cynical that they have out-grown religion, we find many taken in by such frauds.

DEFINITION OF TERMS

Because it is important to know what we are talking about, it's always good to begin with definitions.

Mediums and Channeling:

Listen to how First Spiritual Temple, a spiritualist church, defines these terms and what else it has to say about them:

> Mediumship can be defined as follows: The process whereby a human instrument, known as a MEDIUM or CHANNEL, is used by one or more discarnate, spirit personalities for the purpose(s) of: presenting information, verifiable or otherwise; causing so-called paranormal activities to occur; channeling forth certain types of energies; manifesting themselves for objective examination and/or identification. From this definition, we see the

> following: mediumship involves a cooperating effort between a person on the Earth plane (the medium or channel) and a person in Spirit (the communicator). There are several objectives behind the manifestation of mediumship. In addition to this, we see that mediumship is used by those in Spirit for the following purposes: to present information, which may or may not be verifiable; to cause certain types of paranormal activities to occur; to channel forth certain types of energies; to manifest themselves materially. Thus, mediumship can be distinguished as two basic types: mental mediumship; physical mediumship. Mental mediumship involves the relating of information, through communication, via the varied aspects of thought transference, or mental telepathy. Mental telepathy is the relaying of information via thought, without using any of the five physical senses . . . Physical mediumship involves the manipulation and transformation of physical systems and energies. The spirit operators, in this case, are causing something to happen upon the Earth plane. What it is that actually happens varies with the style of mediumship involved, but the results can be seen and heard by others" ("Medium").

Such a long quotation, defining these things from the viewpoint of those who claim to believe in such things will be, I believe, helpful.

Apport: This is the materializing of objects during a seance. Any good magician is able to duplicate such.

Clairvoyance: The supposed (pretended) ability to see things without the use of the physical senses.

Clairaudience: The supposed (pretended) ability to hear things without the use of the physical senses.

Telekinesis: The supposed (pretended) ability to move things with the power of the mind.

Psychokinesis: The supposed (pretended) production of things by the power of the mind.

Spiritualism: The belief that the personality lives on after death and can communicate in various ways with the living, usually through someone called a medium or a channeler.

Seance: A meeting of spiritualists in order to bring up departed spirits for the purpose of communicating with them. This may be done by the medium or channeler speaking in a strange voice claiming to be the voice of the departed spirit. It used to be common to have physical manifestations (by trickery) of figures, raps, or tables levitating.

THE ORIGINS OF MEDIUMS AND CHANNELING

Although mediums have been here for a long time, channeling only got started with the publication of the book by Jane Roberts and Robert Butts, her husband, entitled Seth Speaks. This was in 1972. They claimed that "Seth" spoke through Jane who then dictated what he said to Robert. In order to make her claims more believable, her defenders say that what she said was beyond her capacity to concoct. The truth is that she was a highly literate person, studied in the occult, and an accomplished poet.

Many channelers speak in an assumed voice with a foreign accent to make it seem as though another person is speaking through them. According to her book, Out on a Limb, Ryerson, one of Shirley MacLaine's favorite channelers, claims that "John," who lived at the time of Christ, speaks through him. Instead of speaking in Aramaic, the language that John likely used, he speaks a sort of 16th Century English. He has informed Shirley MacLaine that she helped God create the world!

In order to supposedly produce physical phemenoma, many mediums or channelers pretend to enter a trance state. Listen to what they have to say:

> "Trance is considered the strongest degree of control. Yet, even here, there are various degrees of trance control: from light trance to very deep trance. Deep trance is used primarily in physical mediumship . . . There is generally--although not always--manifested, within the medium, the following: A slowing of the heart rate; A slow, deep, and steady breathing pattern; No rapid eye movement, or REM; A lowering of body temperature; A greatly reduced reaction to touch and pain; Various degrees of unconsciousness" ("Trance").

All of these signs may be exhibited by someone who is conscious and fully in control of self, although the fourth and fifth items will take practice. But who is likely to take the temperature of or inflict pain upon their channeler?

PHYSICAL MEDIUMSHIP

Listen to this quote from the First Spiritual Temple: "During the last century, up until around the 1930's, physical mediumship was very common, and the strength and range of phenomena were amazing. Today, it is quite rare." "Physical mediumship" is rare these days, because magicians in the past exposed these things as common tricks. Men like Harry Houdini and Joseph Dunninger devoted a great deal of their time and expertise in showing that these so-called mediums were frauds and con-men. When one looks at the so-called evidence for such physical phenomena, it almost wholly consists of old photographs (from the early part of this century), before trick photography was well known.

Many of the photographs are the result of double-exposures. Other pictures of "ectoplasm," a ghostly substance seen at times oozing from the nose or nostrils of the mediums, or at other times supposedly becoming fifth legs to a table, is nothing but moistened cheesecloth in a mostly darkened room.

Sir Arthur Conan Doyle, the creator of Sherlock Holmes, was a firm believer in spiritualism. One thing that reinforced his belief was the photographs that two teenage girls took in 1917 of fairies in their garden in Yorkshire, England.

> "Elsie Wright (age 16) and her cousin Francis Griffiths (age 10) used a simple camera and were said to be lacking any knowledge of photography or photographic trickery. Photo No. I, taken in July, showed Frances in the garden with a waterfall in the background and a bush in the foreground. Four fairies are dancing upon the bush. Three have wings and one is playing a long flute-like instrument. Frances is not looking at the fairies just in front of her, but seems to be posing for the camera. Photo No. 2, taken in September, showed Elsie sitting on the lawn reaching out her hand to a friendly gnome (about a foot high, with wings) who is stepping forward onto the hem of her wide skirt. Photographic experts who were consulted declared that the negatives had not been tampered with, there was no evidence of double exposures, and that a slight blurring of one of the fairies in photo number one indicated the fairy was moving . . . They seemed not to even entertain the simpler explanation that the fairies were simple paper cutouts fastened on the bush, jiggling slightly in the breeze. Doyle and other believers were also not troubled by the fact that the fairy's wings never showed blurred movement, even

> in the picture of the fairy calmly posed standing in mid-air. Apparently fairy wings don't work like hummingbird's wings. Hardly anyone can look at these photos today and accept them as anything but fakes. The lighting on the fairies does not match that of the girls. The fairy figures have a flat, cutout appearance. But spiritualists, and others, who prefer a world of magic and fantasy, accepted the photos as genuine evidence for fairies . . . Over the years the mystery persisted . . . When the girls (as adults) were interviewed, their responses were evasive. In a BBC broadcast interview in 1975 Elsie said: "I've told you that they're photographs of figments of our imagination and that's what I'm sticking to." In 1977 Fred Gettings stumbled on important evidence while working on a study of early nineteenth-century book illustrations. He found drawings by Claude A. Sheperson in a 1915 children's book which the girls could easily have possessed, and which were without a doubt, the models for the fairies which appeared in the photos. In 1982 the girls admitted, in interviews with Joe Cooper, that they had faked four of the photos. As many had suspected all along, the girls had used paper cutouts of fairy drawings . . . On the matter of Conan Doyle's gullibility, Gilbert Chesterton said, "It has long seemed to me that Sir Arthur's mentality is much more that of Watson that it is of Holmes" (Doyle).

Recently a number of new "ghost" photographs hit the Western world. They showed a strange, ghostly white shape across the photograph that was not the result of double exposure or cutouts. These shapes were found in both black and white and color photographs. Some people appeared on TV with these photos and Fate magazine even sponsored a nationwide ghost photo contest. These strange forms appeared in all six winning photos. It was finally discovered that these forms were nothing more than the camera strap getting in front of the lens of the camera (either accidentally or on purpose). Actually any string will do. This is what produced the "ghostly" photographs.

THE BEGINNINGS OF SPIRITUALISM

How did spiritualism and belief in mediums and channelers get started? Believe or not, it all started with a prank by pre-teenage girls, Margaret and Kate Fox, March 31, 1848, (the day before April Fool's Day). This took place in Hydesville, New York, about 20 miles from Rochester. This prank was so exploited by their sister, Mrs. Daniel Underhill (then Mrs. Fish) who was much older than they, that for years afterward they traveled the great cities of the world as genuine mediums. The spiritualist churches, first formed by their older sister, and the movement of today, traces its origins to them and still hails them as genuine.

But on October 21, 1888, Margaret Fox, whose younger sister Kate had by then died, gave the New York World an interview in which she confessed that it had all been a fraud. It had begun that night by the girls, ages eight and six, wanting to frighten their superstitious mother by bumping an apple tied to a string up and down on the floor after they had gone to bed in their second story bedroom. When their mother came to investigate, they pretended to be asleep. The mother soon concluded that her daughters were "haunted." She called the neighbors in and told them. Soon so many people were coming to the house that they had to find another way to make the raps. That was when they discovered that they could produce rapping noise with the knuckles of the toes of their feet. They practiced until they could do this easily when the room was dark. Margaret said that their older sister knowingly encouraged their trickery. Their mother by her credulous reaction encouraged their fun.

As they grew up, their older sister exploited them, their notoriety, and their ability to make raps with their toes. In time they both became alcoholics. Thus, spiritualism, mediumship, and channeling got its start.

JAMES VAN PRAAGH

The best-known medium or channeler of this present day is probably James Van Praagh. He can be often seen on television. In fact, I have seen him just this past week on the Charles Grodin show, July 10, 1999. He has also appeared on "The Joan Rivers Show," "The Other Side," "The Mo Show," [?] "Maury Povich," "Larry King Live," and "Paranormal Borderline."

He has done almost a hundred radio and newspaper interviews. He has a book out with the title Talking to Heaven. (Somehow, I doubt it. It would be better if he would let heaven talk to him.) The exposure and publicity he receives on TV and radio continue to provide him with paying clients. You currently have to stand in line three years to have a private session with James Van Praagh. The Skeptics Dictionary has this to say in its article on James Van Praagh:

> "He plays a kind of twenty-questions game with his audience. He goes fishing, rapidly casting his baited questions one after the other until he gets a bite. Then he reels the fish in. Sometimes he falters, but most of the fish don't get away. He just rebaits and goes after the fish again until he rehooks. The fish love it. When he can't get a good bite, he reminds his audience that sometimes the message is in fragments, sometimes he doesn't understand it,

> sometimes he misinterprets it, etc. If he's wrong, don't blame him since he never claimed to be perfect. . . What saves him much of the time are ambiguous questions that end with "am I right?" and the client saying "yes," though we have no idea what the "yes" is in response to. Is he sincere in what he does? Is he self-deceived or is he a deceiver?"

Listen to what the experts have to say:

> "I contacted numerous mentalists [magicians who specialize in mindreading tricks--D.C.] about Van Praagh and they all assure me, without reservation, that it would be impossible for him to be self-deceiving because these are techniques that they all use and do so consciously and purposefully. I was told that I was being naive in trying to give Van Praagh the benefit of the doubt. I even talked to someone I know who works a 900-psychic hotline, who is a skeptic but believes there might be somethings to "some" psychic abilities. It turns out he knows James Van Praagh, and many of the people who work with him in that industry . . . and he assures me that Van Praagh is not self-deceived. The psychic industry consensus, this source tells me, is that James Van Praagh knows exactly what he is doing" (Rice).

He has several times been caught cheating. One time on 20/20 he told a woman, "There is a lady sitting behind you. She feels like a grandmother to me." Many were impressed with this "hit." But 54 minutes earlier, film showed that he had gotten the information from this woman that her grandmother had died (Rice). Another time a producer of NBC's program The Other Side, told how Van Praagh had earlier asked about the profession of one of the dead relatives of one of the guests on the program. The producer told him he was a fireman.

Later in the show he said, "I see a uniform. Was he a policeman or fireman, please?" All were impressed by his psychic ability, even though he had access to this information ahead of time (Rice). Michael Shermer tells of an appearance Van Praagh made on a local NBC affiliate in Denver. Again he was exposed on film. Before beginning the on-air reading, he said he had to make a bathroom visit. As he went past the subject to be interviewed (having been told she had lost her sister) he softly asked her what her sister's name was. She replied, "Jan." About ten minutes into the reading, he asks, "Is your sister's name Jan or Janet, please?" (Praagh 4). No wonder Roy Rivenburg of the *Los Angeles Times* has dubbed him, James Van Fraud!

Van Praagh, like most fraudulent (as well as entertainment) mentalists, uses three basic methods of reading:

1. "***Cold Reading***. Most of what Van Praagh does is what is known in the mentalism trade as cold reading, where you literally "read" someone "cold,"--knowing nothing about them. He asks lots of questions and makes numerous statements, some general and some specific, and sees what sticks. Most of the time he is wrong. His subjects visibly [shake] their heads "no." But, . . . he only needs an occasional hit to convince his clientele he is genuine. Sometimes he gets lucky, and as mentalists note, you always take credit for lucky hits.
2. ***Warm Reading***. This is utilizing known principles of psychology that apply to nearly everyone. For example, most grieving women will wear a piece of jewelry that has a connection to their loved one . . . Van Praagh knows this about mourning people and will say something like "do you have a ring or a piece of jewelry on you, please?" His subject cannot believe her

ears and nods enthusiastically in the affirmative. He says "thank you," and moves on like he just divined this from heaven. Most people also keep a photograph of their loved one either on them or near their bed, and Van Praagh will take credit for this specific hit that actually applies to most people. He is clever at determining the cause of death by focusing either on the chest or head areas, and then exploring whether it was a slow or sudden end . . . Statistically speaking there are only half a dozen ways 90% of us die, so with just a little probing, and the verbal and nonverbal cues of his subject, he can appear to get far more hits here than he is really getting.

3. ***Hot Reading***. Mentalist Max Maven clarified for me that some mentalists and psychics also do "hot" readings, where they obtain information on a subject ahead of time. I do not know if Van Praagh uses private detectives to get information on people, but I have discovered from numerous television producers who were less than impressed by the medium, that Van Praagh consciously and deliberately pumps them for information about his subjects ahead of time, then uses that information to deceive the viewing public that he got it from the spirit world" (Praagh 2).

JAMES RANDI

Probably the best-known foe of fraudulent mediums and channelers (as well as other false claimants of occult powers) is James Randi. He is a professional magician who originally specialized in escapes and mental magic, but has in the last thirty years spent his efforts in investigating and exposing false claims of occultic quacks. He was born as Randall James Hamilton Zwinge in 1928 in Toronto, Canada, but has since had his name legally changed to James Randi. He has an IQ of 168, which is genius level. He is a skeptic of any claims of the supernatural.

His best known case of exposure is probably that of self-proclaimed psychic, Uri Geller. On television Randi has both explained and duplicated Geller's "psychic" ability and such claimed psychokenetic ability as spoon-bending and clock-stopping.

In 1986 Randi exposed TV "miracle worker" Peter Popoff. Popoff went through his audience stopping at various people, claiming to receive messages from God, Who supposedly told him about that person's problems. They did not know that Popoff's wife had received the information from those who had spoken to those people as they were waiting to enter the auditorium. She then relayed this information to Popoff by radio as he spoke to the people during the program. He picked it up by a tiny speaker hidden in his ear. Randi discovered the frequency on which she was operating, taped it, and played it, along with Popoff's claimed "revelations" from God. As a result Popoff declared bankruptcy, but now is back on the air. Oh, how quickly people forget!

Randi has offered $1,000,000 to anyone who can demonstrate under scientifically controlled circumstances psychic abilities. Although 77 have been tested, no one has won the money.

I want to include a rather long quote from a speech given by Randi because it illustrates, better than I could, the principles by which the practitioners of the occult operate.

> "I am in a very peculiar business. I appear on stages around the world as a conjurer. Now the American term for it is magician. It's not a good expression because if you look in

the dictionary the strict definition of a magician is one who uses magic. And magic, at least by the definition I prefer from a leading dictionary, is the attempt to control nature by means of spells and incantations. Now, ladies and gentlemen, in my time, as you might have guessed, I have tried spells and incantations. No good. You can spell and incant all you want; the lady will still be on the couch, waiting patiently to float into the air or will be imprisoned in the box with the saw blade descending upon her unprotected midriff, and in some danger of being severely scratched, if not worse! Spells and incantations don't work. You have to use skullduggery. And let me make it very clear what the magical trade--the conjuring trade--is with a precise definition, It is the approximation of the effect of a true magician using means of subterfuge and trickery. There is a hunger, a very strong hunger, within us all to believe there is something more than what the laws of nature permit. I'm not just saying audiences that watch the magician. I mean with us all. We'd like to have a certain amount of fantasy in our lives, but it's a very dangerous sort of temptation to immediately assume that it must be the supernatural or occult or paranormal if we don't have an explanation for it. I can tell you that in my life I've spent a great deal of time investigating and observing and carefully noting and making use of psychology. I am not a psychologist; I have no academic credentials whatsoever, so I come to you today absolutely unencumbered by any responsibilities of that nature. There is no dean who will call me on the carpet tomorrow morning and say, "You shouldn't have said that." You see, I'm in the business of giving opinions from an uninformed point of view, except from the point of view of a skeptical person who knows how people's minds work and often don't work.... [He then talks about the role that the news media plays in the acceptance of the occult.] For example, a few years ago the New York Daily News, on page three where they put the "heavy news" and sensational stuff, announced that a student at Duke University had successfully in great detail described not only an aircraft accident 24 hours in advance of the event, he even gave the number of people who would be killed. He was short by only two. He even described the location of the crash in the Canary Islands. That was picked up by news services and was featured on television programs; it was on every newscast for quite some time. It was received by the press as a genuine example of prophecy, and the director of the program in which this was involved at Duke University actually made a statement that he had a sealed envelope 24 hours before in his safe that was not touched by this gentleman until after the episode had taken place. It was allegedly torn open at that time and it contained the prediction. To explain this phenomena I will take you into a different world, for just a moment, so you will understand something. Magicians know how this young man could very easily have done this trick. I won't go into all the details; you can imagine some of them yourself. But the effect is exactly as described--a sealed signed envelope, put into a safe, later carefully opened. Inside you either find a tape cassette or a sealed letter with all kinds of security on it, signed, maybe genuinely notarized, as of the day before. It contains the prediction. A miracle of a semi-religious nature? No, it's a trick. Any good magician can do it. Now, let us return to the article in the Daily News, first edition. It came out in the afternoon. It had the story on page 3, and a box in the middle of it describing the mechanics of how it had been locked up in a safe and it had a final paragraph which quoted the student at Duke University who made the prediction with this disclaimer: "It's all part of the publicity for my magic show, which is happening tomorrow night. Don't take it seriously." The second and third editions of the Daily News had everything except that one sentence. [This incident is very similar to the one that I relate in the article in this book entitled "Black Magic."]

Another example of how the media distorts claims comes from a young fellow who lived a few doors down from me when I was living in Rumson, New Jersey. He was one of the local characters who did adventurous things like going out on rafts and sailboats. I thought he was a nice kid. One day on the front page of the New York Times there was a little box showing a map of the Bermuda Triangle with a Maltese Cross on it. The headline read: "Rumson boy lost at sea in Bermuda Triangle.: I read the short article, continued on another page, which said he had taken off in his one-man sailboat, sailed into the Triangle carrying a radio transmitter, and hadn't been heard from since. The Coast Guard was searching for him. No sooner had I finished reading this and had called some friends in New York to tell them about it, I went out to pick up the mail and to my shock there was this kid waving hello to me. He was perfectly all right! I said to him, "You're in the Times this morning." He said, "Yeah, they picked me up late last night and they brought me in.

> They want me to be observed in the hospital, but I feel perfectly all right. We had a bit of a storm; I lost the radio overboard and they finally picked me up very, very early, around 2:30 this morning and they flew me in." Though the first story made a big splash, the followup never appeared in the New York Times or any other paper of which I know. It's still part of the mythology about the Bermuda Triangle. So far as we know, from reading accounts that published in newspapers, that kid is still someplace out in a sailboat in the Bermuda Triangle or perhaps taken off to Mars. You've got to learn that newspaper editors and reporters are subject to the same kinds of pressures that we all are. We all want something successful. Often the choice is between a story and a non-story. We have to realize that we cannot depend on the media to always represent the facts as they actually are . . . Be careful about accepting what appears in print; don't let them say to you, "They put it in the paper; it must be so," or "Someone wrote a book on it, It must be so" (Randi).

WHY SUCH WIDE-SPREAD BELIEF IN THE OCCULT?

There are a number of reasons that many people are gullible enough to swallow the nonsense of the occult - more than I can cover in this article.

The fact is that many people want to believe it. As a result, some are going to, no matter what the evidence says. This is known as wishful thinking - wanting something to be true and so interpreting incidents that we hear about or read about according to our prejudices or wishes.

The basis for most acceptance of occultic phenomena, including that of the medium or channeler, is selective thinking. Listen to the following example:

> "Peter Hurkos was astonishing people with his ability to recite intimate details about their homes and their lives. Two of the persons whom had their minds read by Hurkos and who were amazed at his accuracy were invited by Randi to watch a tape of the mind readings. It was "discovered by actual count that this so-called psychic had, on the average, been correct in one out of fourteen of his statements.... Selective thinking had led them to dismiss all the apparent misses and the obviously wrong guesses and remember only the 'hits.' They were believers who needed this man to be the genuine article, and in spite of the results of this experiment they are still devoted fans of this charlatan" (Carroll).

People also ascribe psychic power to others because of subjective validation. By subjective validation I mean taking statements that could be applied to anyone and applying them to ourselves. For instance, if I gave the following reading, it could very well apply to anyone:

"You are a capable person although you have some self-doubts that are hidden from the outside world. Finances are not as smooth as you would like them to be, but will improve in the future. You have a certain attraction to those of the opposite sex, but you want to be careful. You are in reasonably good health, but there is some sickness in your future and accidents that you should do your best to avoid. Your psychic abilities are above average, although you have made a few mistakes in judgment about people. You are a likeable person and make friends fairly easily, but you have a few enemies that you should watch and be careful of although you seem to be controlled, you have some unresolved inner conflicts and self-doubts. Your opinions are your own, and you do not form them without adequate evidence. The immediate future for you looks good. You will soon have a change in your life for the better."

We tend to take general statements like these, especially if they are delivered with confidence, and apply them to ourselves. This is how professional psychics, mediums, and channelers work.

WHAT DOES THE BIBLE SAY?

Although the Bible does not mention mediums and channeling by those names, it does condemn that activity. "Thou shalt not suffer a sorceress to live," (Exodus 22:18). "Ye shall not eat anything with the blood: neither shall ye use enchantments, nor practice augury... Turn ye not unto them that have familiar spirits, nor unto the wizards; seek them not out, to be defiled by them: Lam Jehovah your God," (Leviticus 19:26, 31). "And the soul that turneth unto them that have familiar spirits, and unto the wizards, to play the harlot after them, I will even set my face against that soul, and will cut him off from among his people," (Leviticus 20:6). "And when they shall say unto you, Seek unto them that have familiar spirits and unto the wizards, that chirp and that mutter: should not a people seek unto their God? on behalf of the living should they seek unto the dead? To the law and to the testimony! if they speak not according to this word, surely there is no morning for them," (Isaiah 8:19-20). In the New Testament we read, "But for the fearful, and unbelieving, and abominable, and murderers, and fornicators, and sorcerers, and idolaters, and all liars, their part shall be in the lake that burneth with fire and brimstone; which is the second death" (Revelation 2 1:8).

Mediumship and channeling are not only instances of fraud and trickery, they are contrary to the Word of God. They are products of the devil and poor imitations of the power and reality of God Almighty. Their obvious falsity helps to promote unbelief in that which is true and right. Let us be obedient to what Paul said in 1 Thessalonians 5:21: "Prove all things; hold fast that which is good."

WORKS CITED

Carroll, Robert Todd. The Skeptics Dictionary. http://skepdic.com/slectiv.html

Doyle, Arthur Conan. Spiritualism, and Fairies. http://www.lhup.edu/~dsimanek/doyle.htm

"Medium." The First Spiritual Temple. http://www.fst.org/medium.htm

"Physmed." The First Spiritual Temple. http://www.fst.org/physmed.htm

"Praagh 2." Michael Shermer. http://www.holysmoke.org/skeptic-tank/praagh2.htm

"Praagh 4." Michael Shermer. http://www.holysmoke.org/skeptic-tank/praagh4.htm

Rice, Fredrick L. http://www.holysmoke.org/skeptic-tank/praagh.htm

"Trance." The First Spiritual Temple. http://www.fst.org/trance.htm